DISASTER!

THREE REAL-LIFE STORIES OF SURVIVAL

Ellen Leroe

HYPERION BOOKS FOR CHILDREN

NEW YORK

Dedicated with love to Bernard W. Leroe
and Walter Marks:
Always in our thoughts;
forever in our hearts

Printed in the United States of America
First Edition
1 3 5 7 9 10 8 6 4 2
The text for this book is set in Cheltenham 12/17.

Library of Congress Cataloging-in-Publication data
Leroe, Ellen, 1949-
Disaster!: three real-life stories of survival / Ellen Leroe— 1st ed.
                    p.   cm.
Summary: First-person survivor accounts of three disasters:
the 1914 shipwreck of the *Empress of Ireland*, the 1928 crash
of the airship *Italia*, and the 1930 crash of the dirigible R-101.
ISBN 0-7868-1403-9 (paperback) — ISBN 0-7868-2474-3 (library)
1. Survival after airplane accidents, shipwrecks, etc.—Juvenile literature.
2. Disasters—Juvenile literature. [1. Survival. 2. Disasters. 3. Airships.
4. Shipwrecks.] I. Title.
TL553.7 .L47 2000
363.12'4—dc21
99-45197

Contents

Preface

A luxury transatlantic crossing, a noted scientific expedition to the North Pole, the maiden voyage of the world's largest dirigible: all three ventures began in a state of high hopes, anticipation, and excitement. But all too soon adventure turned into misadventure when the unthinkable happened. By bringing together recountings of real-life dramas, *Disaster!* reveals uplifting truths about human nature in the face of adversity.

When the unthinkable happens, not everyone is a hero. Confronted by the sudden and shocking threat of death, individuals react in a variety of ways, not always courageously or morally. Panic and fear too often dominate the emotions of those thrown into the ultimate crisis. But weakness of character isn't about being afraid. Openly expressing fear and acting in spite of it reveal true strength of character and mark the survivor as belonging to a breed apart.

In each of the following remarkable true stories, men and women performed acts of daring in the middle of terrible, paralyzing fear. They struggled to stay alive, yet risked their lives to help others. They worked together when secretly they wanted to give up.

More than a collection of thrilling historical adventures, *Disaster!* is a testament of courage and determination—the stories of individuals who wrestled with their fears, as well as the elements, and endured.

The Death of the *Empress*

*The sinking of the
Canadian Pacific liner*
Empress of Ireland,

May 28, 1914

On the evening of April 14, 1912, at 11:40 P.M., the largest, and supposedly safest, British ship of its day struck an iceberg and sank, killing 807 passengers and 695 of its crew. Of course, everyone has heard the tragic story of the *Titanic*. It's one of the most publicized and well-known disasters of the twentieth century.

But just two years later, on May 28, 1914, another huge ocean liner making an Atlantic crossing sailed to her doom. On that fateful night, when the liner sank in just fourteen minutes on the fog-enshrouded St. Lawrence River, one of the survivors became a nationally recognized hero, while another survivor lost a member of her family in one of the worst maritime disasters ever. This is their story.

Setting Off

"Stay close now, Tiria. I don't want to lose you."

Tiria Townshend turned to see her aunt Wynnie Price motioning to her on the landing dock. Hoping no one had overhead, Tiria quickly moved to her aunt's side.

"I'm not a baby," she told her aunt with an embarrassed look. "I'm seventeen, not seven, and taller than most everyone here. Besides, how can you miss me in my newest creation?"

Tilting her head, Tiria proudly struck a pose in the flared-brim hat that barely restrained her springy auburn hair. With its silk rosettes and genuine ostrich quills, the hat was the height of fashion in 1914. Tiria felt elegant and grown-up wearing it, just as she felt elegant and grown-up in her new flared, ankle-length jumper dress, ruffled blouse, and cutaway jacket joined by mother-of-pearl buttons.

But Aunt Wynnie shook her head in concern.

"Just stick close, my girl. I can barely see you in this crush."

Aunt Wynnie had a point, Tiria realized, as she felt herself being pushed from behind. The landing dock in Quebec City on the Gulf of Saint Lawrencewas swarming with people of all shapes, sizes, and nationalities, standing in line to board the *Empress of Ireland*. If Tiria failed to pay proper attention, she'd lose sight of tiny, plump Aunt Wynnie in a second. At this stage of her trip, she didn't want anything to go wrong. She and Aunt Wynnie had just endured a long steamship crossing from their home-town of Blenheim, New Zealand. They had docked in Los Angeles, before traveling by train across the Rockies to reach Quebec. From here they'd be sailing on the *Empress of Ireland* to Liverpool, England, for the first stop on a grand European tour.

Tiria couldn't wait to explore England, France, and Germany, but there were times she was home-sick. She missed her friends and family. She missed life on her parents' sprawling twelve-acre sheep ranch, riding horses in the outback, canoeing, and swimming. She especially missed her favorite col-lies, Jiggs and Peanut. In two months I'll be home, she thought. And what exciting adventures I'll have to share with my friends!

The line for first-class passengers began moving,

interrupting her thoughts, and her aunt nudged her forward.

"It's a beautiful ship, isn't it?" Aunt Wynnie asked. "The largest and fastest Canadian liner to cross the Atlantic."

Tiria took a moment to crane her head and look up at the gleaming side of the ship. The *Empress of Ireland* was a long ocean liner with a straight stem, shiny black sides, and two high buff funnels with black tops. Wisps of smoke curled from her funnels, and the red-and-white checkered flag of the Canadian Pacific Railway Company fluttered in the late afternoon May breeze.

It was funny, Tiria thought, heading up the gangplank. When her parents had booked passage on the *Empress* for Tiria and her aunt, she had never imagined a ship of this size sailing from a *river*. But her father had explained that this river, the Saint Lawrence, was more like a small sea. It ran seven hundred miles from end to end between the deep Atlantic Ocean and the Quebec countryside, and was nearly twenty-five miles across at its most narrow part.

"Am I boring you with all these facts?" Mr. Townshend had said, but Tiria had smiled.

"I don't get bored easily," she had replied. "Nothing bores me and nothing frightens me.

You know that."

It was a joke in her family that Tiria, the eldest child and only daughter, was always looking for adventure and excitement, while her four younger brothers were the quiet, well-behaved ones.

"Just you listen to Aunt Wynn and don't get into any mischief," Mrs. Townshend had cautioned Tiria before she embarked on the sturdy, if dull, Canadian Pacific steamer from New Zealand. "Someday your impulsiveness is going to get you into trouble."

Tiria absently adjusted her hat, remembering the last time she had seen her mother. It had been days . . . no, a week or more. Suddenly her mother and her entire family seemed a million miles away. An aching desire to see her parents washed over her. "Oh, grow up," she whispered, as she felt her lower lip begin to tremble. Next thing she knew she'd be asking Aunt Wynnie to buy her a doll to help get over her homesickness! Smiling wryly at this image, Tiria followed her aunt on board and stepped into an elegant-looking reception area filled with potted palms and paneled in rich mahogany. A five piece string orchestra sat in a corner, entertaining the first-class passengers with lively Gilbert and Sullivan melodies. Tiria eagerly took in her surroundings. She hadn't managed to get into any mischief yet, but the *Empress of Ireland* seemed to promise an adventure.

Now if only her aunt would stop hovering over her as if she were a baby and allow her to go exploring on her own.

"Oh, look, Tiria," Aunt Wynnie suddenly whispered, "here's the list of all the other first-class passengers who are traveling with us. I hope there are some well-known people on board."

Tiria hid a smile as her aunt leaned down to scan the list. Aunt Wynnie and her never-ending search for famous rail- and shipmates always made Tiria giggle. So far there hadn't been any notable personages on board the steamship or endless train ride, but maybe Aunt Wynnie would get lucky on this crossing.

A uniformed stewardess approached them and introduced herself as Erna Kent. Like everyone else on the *Empress*, she had an English accent. "May I help you find your stateroom?"

The two porters who carried their trunks promised to follow as soon as the crowd thinned out. The stewardess led the way up to the promenade deck and showed Aunt Wynnie her room. While she was exclaiming over the wall paintings and brocaded bed coverlet, the stewardess took Tiria down the hall and showed her another stateroom. It was a two-room suite, spacious and elegantly decorated, with mahogany paneling, and an ornate dressing table and bed. Tiria exclaimed in delight over the ruffled floral curtains and two large portholes.

"And this can be your suite, if you want," the stewardess told a surprised Tiria. "First class is less than one third full, so all these rooms are unoccupied."

Tiria flew back to her aunt, who was directing the porters with the steamer trunks.

"Oh, Aunt Wynnie, can I have my own room?" Tiria said. "Miss Kent says I can take an unoccupied suite only a few doors away."

Aunt Wynnie looked up absentmindedly from sorting the luggage.

"*May* I, dear," she automatically corrected, then frowned. "I don't know if that's such a good idea, you and I being separated at night on a ship this size. Why, anything could happen," Aunt Wynnie said.

"Oh, Aunt Wynnie . . ." Tiria complained.

The stewardess gave Tiria a sympathetic smile, then turned to her aunt.

"The *Empress* is one of the safest, most solid passenger liners crossing the ocean today," she explained. "She and her sister ship, the *Empress of Britain*, were built by the Fairchild Shipbuilding Company, one of the greatest names in British shipbuilding. The two sisters are the biggest ships they've built so far, over five hundred fifty feet long."

Aunt Wynnie bit her lip, still looking uncertain.

"Besides," the stewardess continued, "Captain Kendall is one of the most admired and respected seamen on both sides of the Atlantic. He's been sailing for over twenty-five years and never lost a passenger yet."

"You see, Aunt Wynnie," Tiria burst out. "I'll be perfectly fine on my own. Nothing's going to go wrong on a ship like the *Empress*."

"Is there a problem?"

A uniformed steward of considerable size and with an air of authority peered in at them from the doorway. Although his Scottish brogue sounded gruff, his eyes twinkled in a friendly manner.

"Oh, Chief Steward Gaade," the stewardess said. "I was just explaining to Aunt Wynnie and her niece, Miss Townshend, that the *Empress of Ireland* is as safe as a luxury hotel and that's there no reason why Miss Townshend shouldn't have the pleasure of staying in her own stateroom during the sailing."

"I'm Augustus Gaade," the burly officer nodded to both Aunt Wynnie and Tiria, "and I'm responsible for seeing that your crossing is as smooth and worry-free as possible. What Miss Kent says is true. Your niece will be quite safe on this voyage in her own suite."

"I'm sure the *Empress* is as safe and as well built

as you claim," Aunt Wynnie stated, and then hesitated. She lowered her voice so they all had to crane to hear her. "But so was the *Titanic*, was she not?"

Tiria's hopes for her own stateroom plummeted. Although her parents and Aunt Wynnie had never openly discussed the major disaster in front of her, she knew the subject weighed all too heavily on their minds. Just two years before, the world's largest liner, the "unsinkable" *Titanic*, struck an iceberg and went down in the Atlantic on her maiden voyage. Out of 2,207 people on board, only 705 had been saved. The newspapers claimed that an insufficient number of lifeboats was the cause of so many deaths. Her aunt always feared the same would happen to them on their around-the-world travels.

"Aunt Wynnie, we're *not* going to hit an iceberg and sink!" Tiria protested, feeling her cheeks flush with embarrassment.

But Officer Gaarde regarded her aunt seriously. "You raise a good point, madam. Because of what happened to the *Titanic*, the *Empress of Ireland* has lifeboats to spare for over 1,800 people, far more than we'd ever need. Not only that, but we carry more than 2,000 life jackets, all within easy access of the passengers."

"Our crew performs many drills in safety measures," Erna Kent added. "Just yesterday the men swung all the lifeboats out, and then lowered them into the water and rowed about in the Saint Lawrence. Everything worked perfectly."

Officer Gaade beamed at Aunt Wynnie, who was beginning to lose her worried frown.

"To put your mind at rest even further, I want you to know that Captain Staunton sails with us. Captain Staunton is a fine gentleman and the official inspector of boats and lifesaving appliances. He inspects and drills the crew most diligently, so there is nothing to fear."

"Well, I am impressed. It sounds like we *all* will be safe," Aunt Wynnie said, and smiled. "All right, Tiria, you may excuse yourself to go to your room and begin to unpack. But don't dawdle. The ship's about to cast off very shortly."

In a burst of happy spirits, Tiria hurried to her private stateroom and began to unpack. Every so often she'd stop unfolding dresses and blouses to peer out the portholes. The crowds of well-wishers were still clustered on the dock, but the bulk of passengers had already come on board. She pushed open the porthole in her bedroom and took a deep breath. The air was pungent with the reek of coal smoke from the ship's engine and funnels, tangy from the river breezes. It may have offended a more delicate nose, but Tiria drank it all in like a sip of forbidden champagne. Electric cranes whined, sea-gulls wheeled lazily overhead in a sunny, cloudless sky, and the water sparkled in the horizon.

I am so lucky, Tiria thought. I am the luckiest girl on earth.

Just then the ship's whistle blew, startling her. The *Empress of Ireland* was about to depart. Tiria and her aunt hurried on deck to witness the momentous event. Many passengers crowded around them, but Tiria and Aunt Wynnie managed to find space at the railing. The well-wishers and people on shore threw streamers and waved energetically. "Godspeed!" they cried. "Safe journey!" The first-class passengers shouted out names and farewells to those gathered below. To add to the noise and gaiety, a Salvation Army band that had come on board in second class began to serenade the crowd from the promenade deck.

Before the last mooring lines had been cast off, Tiria noticed a scrawny yellow cat dart out of the arms of a steward on ship and scamper down the gangway.

"Oh look, Aunt Wynnie!" Tiria remarked with a giggle, pointing at the cat. "It's trying to escape."

The frantic-looking steward dashed down the gangway to scoop up the cat. With seconds to spare before the ship cast off, he raced back up the gangway with the animal in tow.

"The cat's making another run for it," Tiria exclaimed, as the yellow cat wriggled free once again. It sprinted down the gangway and then darted inside the open door of a freight shed.

The steward threw up his hands and stayed on board. The last mooring line splashed into the Saint Lawrence, and then the liner slid away from the dock. The yellow cat poked its head out of the freight shed and watched the ship depart.

"Poor little thing," Tiria said. "The sound of all the noise and the engine whistles probably frightened him."

She smiled at her aunt, but Aunt Wynnie was frowning, clutching her coat around herself for warmth against a sudden cool breeze from the water.

"Why didn't that cat stay on the ship?" Aunt Wynnie said. Her face puckered in dismay as she turned to face her niece. "Oh, I hope that wasn't an omen for this voyage."

A Smooth Night for Sailing

Ronald Ferguson pushed his unfinished coffee away and stood up. Normally the senior wireless operator enjoyed lingering over dinner in the officers' dining room, but not tonight. He felt impatient to get back to the wireless room and see if everything was all right. His junior partner, Edward Bamford, had graduated from the Marconi Company's school only six months before, and at the age of twenty, hadn't had much experience in sending and receiving messages. Although Eddy showed promise, he still missed occasional signals.

Ronald was only three years older, but he had joined the Marconi Company at Liverpool in 1910 and had quickly taken to the telegraph system. He had sailed on five different ships for the past three years and now was the senior wireless officer on board the *Empress*. Ronald believed in the miracle of the wireless radio completely, even though it was considered a fairly new invention in 1914. He loved everything about it, from the sound of the constant buzz and splutter of the transmittal code to the look of the smart double-breasted uniform and gold-trimmed cap embroidered with the Marconi initial.

Working for the Marconi Company gave him special status aboard the *Empress*, as well. Although his salary was paid by Canadian Pacific, he reported to no officer on the ship. He and Eddy liked to joke that they ruled their little kingdom without having to take orders from anyone. The only time that a Marconi Company operator had to get permission from a ship's officer before acting was in emergency situations. No SOS could be sent without first consulting the captain. But other than that rarely enforced restriction, he and Eddy were on their own. No doubt about it, Ronald congratulated himself as he left the dining room, *I've got the best job in the entire world.* Whistling under his breath, the young operator nodded to several officers as he entered the narrow corridor, and then paused.

He wasn't due to begin his long, six-hour shift until 7 P.M. He had thirty minutes in which to do whatever he wanted, stroll along the officers' promenade or read in the cramped privacy of his bunk.

None of these things appealed to him now. He felt an urgency in returning to the wireless room, a little deckhouse at the stern of the after funnel on the ship. It was a tiny place, yet he and Edward slept and worked comfortably there—one half the living quarters with bunks, the other the radio room. Yet something else prompted him to stick his head out the door leading to the officers' promenade.

The seasonably mild afternoon had lengthened into a clear late spring twilight. Before too long the first-class passengers would be assembling in the dining room on their first night out, and Captain Henry Kendall would leave his responsibilities on the bridge to join them. Ronald breathed in the sea air, then came out on deck. He walked over to the railing and peered down at the churning water. The Saint Lawrence might be called a calm waterway in the travel brochures, but she was cold and deep. Nearly 150 feet deep at this exact point. Ronald never liked admitting it, but he was a little afraid of the ocean. That's why being cooped up in the tiny wireless room for long stretches at a time didn't bother him. He could throw himself into receiving and transmitting messages and forget about the fact that bottomless water, and not solid ground, lay beneath him.

"Don't even think about jumping!"

Startled, Ronald swung around to find Chief Officer Steede laughing at him. Steede, second in command to the captain, must have just come from the bridge.

Relaxing, Ronald laughed, too. Steede could be a stern taskmaster to his men at times, but he was also fair and quick with the jokes when the situation called for it.

"I won't jump," Ronald assured the chief officer. "At least not until my shift's over at one o'clock tonight." He gestured at the calm water gleaming in the moonlight. "Although this voyage is going so smoothly, you might not even need our wireless services."

The stout white-bearded officer joined him at the rail.

"It looks calm," he agreed, "but don't let appearances fool you. The real curse that can spring up at any time is the fog. And this fog over the Saint Lawrence is the worst. The warm air in late April and May meets a river chilled by icy meltwater. You need to be on your toes."

"But it's perfectly clear," Ronald said.

"Take a closer look, my lad."

He followed the chief officer's glance and spotted a drifting patch of fog that moved across the liner's path. Immediately the *Empress* slowed to half speed, the rhythmic drumming of the engines becoming softer. Once the fog had disappeared, the engines picked up again.

"It'll probably be that way all night," Steede

commented. "I wager the captain will be alert and on the bridge until we clear the gulf and enter the ocean."

"But you don't predict any serious trouble, do you?" Ronald needed reassurance from the competent senior officer.

Steede stroked the heavy white beard that gave his face such a commanding appearance.

"The *Empress of Britain* encountered weather like this two years ago. The night seemed clear until fog rolled in. Before anyone could sound the alarm, our sister ship struck a Norwegian coal transporter called the *Helvetia* only twenty miles from this location."

Ronald drew in a nervous breath. "What happened?"

Steede turned away to face the water.

"The *Helvetia* sank," he said shortly. Suddenly the first officer pounded the rail in anger. "It's the fault of the infernal Saint Lawrence and the men who govern her. There are lights and buoys on the southern shore of the river to guide ships, but no individually marked channels to separate ships passing each other."

Seeing Ronald's uneasiness, Steede barked out a laugh. "We'll be fine on this trip, my boy. You wait and see. You and Mr. Bamford take care of business at your end, and let the captain and me take care of ours. We'll get to Liverpool in record time."

Ronald tipped his hat as Steede gave him a jaunty salute and then walked away.

When the sister ship to the *Empress* had collided with the Helvetia vessel, Ronald had been sailing on another ship and had never heard about it. He peered over the rail into the cold black water. A tight uneasy knot formed in his stomach and he took a quick step back.

Fine brave officer you are, he chastised himself with a weak grin. Getting yourself all worked up over something that took place a long time ago. There was nothing to be worried about on this crossing. The night was basically clear, and the *Empress* was making good speed. Yes, there was the hint of fog, but hadn't there been fog on many of his other sailings to England? Nothing had happened then and nothing would happen now. The voyage would be routine and he'd be seeing his parents in Mersey, England, in less than six days.

Regaining his usual good spirits, Ronald quickly navigated the narrow decks and entered the wireless room. His younger partner sat hunched over the radio on the desk, earphones covering his head. With his shock of wiry brown hair and a boyish face, Eddy looked like he was barely out of his teens, while

Ronald prided himself on his own carefully groomed mustache and mature features. Now Ronald saw that Eddy was rubbing his eyes tiredly as he scribbled down messages.

"Anything important come through when I was away?" Ronald asked.

Eddy shook his head and frowned. "*Nothing* important ever comes through. Mostly it's telegrams from our passengers I have to send."

Ronald pulled off his Marconi cap and dropped it on his bunk in the living quarters. Then he reentered the wireless room and faced his junior partner.

"All you ever do is complain, Eddy. You should be happy there's no important news. Too often important or urgent news on a ship like ours means *bad* news."

Eddy sighed and stood up.

"I didn't leave a decent clerk's position at the railroad to transmit boring messages," Eddy grumbled. "If I wanted dull, I would have stayed in England."

He took his earphones off and handed them to Ronald, who promptly put them on and sat down at the desk. Ronald thought about telling Eddy about their sister ship ramming—and sinking—the Norwegian freighter in the Saint Lawrence River, but decided he wouldn't tempt fate. His junior partner was still pretty new at the wireless and this was his very first trip across the Atlantic on the *Empress of Ireland*. No need to pass on a tale that was sad and distressing, and distract Eddy from his duties.

Besides, Ronald thought, as he began to take down an incoming message, a little bit of fog couldn't possibly sink a queen of an ocean liner like the *Empress*.

A Premonition

Dinner for the first-class passengers was served promptly at 7 P.M.

Tiria quickly adjusted the sash around her waist before the gong sounded, and then stepped back to appraise her appearance in the stateroom mirror. The ankle-length navy silk dress was certainly not her prettiest or most fashionable outfit, but Aunt Wynnie made it clear that people didn't dress in their best attire on the first or last night of a voyage. The ruffled rose organdy would have to wait until tomorrow evening, Tiria thought wistfully. She licked her lips, then smoothed back a stray auburn hair. No need to pinch her cheeks for color, because anticipation over this upcoming social event gave her face a natural blush.

When Aunt Wynnie tapped at her door, anxious to be off, Tiria was more than ready.

"Oh, Aunt Wynnie, it's magnificent!" Tiria

whispered, as she and her aunt paused in the entrance to the first-class dining saloon. Situated on the shelter deck, right in the very center of the ship, the saloon was the most elegant sight Tiria had ever seen. Beneath a baroque dome of filtered light, white-and-gold accented walls and columns served as a backdrop to plushly upholstered leather banquettes. Tables for eight were draped in dazzling white linen, set with china plates, gleaming silver, and vases of freshly cut flowers. An orchestra softly played waltzes in the background, while a uniformed steward greeted passengers by name and led them to their appointed tables.

Aunt Wynnie tightened her grip on Tiria's arm. "Oh, I hope we get to sit with some *interesting* individuals!"

By interesting her aunt meant famous, Tiria realized with a smile. But she, too, secretly hoped they'd have the pleasure of some lively dinner companions on their first night out. When the steward greeted them and murmured, "You'll be sitting at the captain's table," both Tiria and her aunt softly exclaimed in unison.

It got even better when the captain, handsome and dashing in his starched white uniform, stood at their approach and introduced them to the other guests already sitting at the table: "This is Mr. and

Mrs. Laurence Irving; their friends and fellow members of the acting troupe, Harold Neville and his wife, Else Vron; and Mr. Clayton Burt."

Laurence Irving, a handsome, soulful-eyed man in his early forties, was a dazzling British actor. His wife, Mabel, was equally as attractive and a famous actress in her own right. Tiria couldn't believe their good fortune in being asked to dine at this table.

"We are surrounded by celebrities," Aunt Wynnie said in delight.

Everyone laughed as they resumed their places, but Captain Kendall playfully shook his head. "I fear I don't fall into that exalted category, Mrs. Price."

Clayton Burt, a big burly man with a bushy handlebar mustache, immediately rose to his feet in good-natured rebuttal. "I cannot agree, sir. You are known to many thousands of people on both sides of the Atlantic for your daring involvement in the capture of Crippen less than four years ago."

"Who is this man Crippen?" Aunt Wynnie said. "You must forgive my ignorance, but I come from New Zealand."

"Hawely Harvey Crippen was a mild-mannered dentist who brutally murdered his wife," Clayton Burt explained, resuming his seat, "and then posed as a passenger on one of Captain Kendall's ships. His disguise fooled everyone else, but it didn't fool our clever captain for long. When he recognized Crippen as the murderer, he alerted Scotland Yard and worked with them to catch the most notorious killer of our time."

"Mercy," Aunt Wynnie murmured in shocked relish. "You *are* a person of note."

"It is the Irvings who are the true celebrities," Captain Kendall insisted. "They should regale us with stories of their triumphs on stage."

When dinner was served nearly an hour later, Tiria barely tasted the roast beef, the grilled mutton chops, or the baked jacketed potatoes. She was entranced by the conversation swirling around her, and especially fascinated by the Irvings. The couple had anecdotes and stories to tell that held everyone spellbound.

The only gloomy note in the entire evening sounded later in the meal, when dessert and coffee were served. Irving put down her china cup and began talking about the mulelike behavior of her maid, who had been vehemently opposed to sailing on the *Empress of Ireland*.

"I practically had to force the poor woman into joining me, and not take the later sailing ship, the *Teutonic*."

"Why didn't she want to sail on this ship?" Tiria said.

Mrs. Irving raised a disdainful eyebrow. "A premonition, if you can believe that. Of all the childish nonsense."

Everyone laughed, but Aunt Wynnie was regarding Mabel Irving with a tense expression.

Oh, no, Tiria thought, glancing across at her aunt. Aunt Wynnie is worried enough about making these transatlantic crossings without having to hear other people's upsetting fears.

"Darling, no need to repeat such foolishness," Laurence Irving suggested, lightly tapping his wife's shoulder. But the actress was too caught up in the story to heed his words.

"My maid says she dreamed a week ago that the *Empress* sank—"

"Oh, no!" Aunt Wynnie blurted, raising a hand to her lips.

"—and now she refuses to sleep a wink on this trip."

Observing Aunt Wynnie's distress, Captain Kendall immediately plunged into an amusing account of an incident that had taken place on board one of his previous ships. Tiria shot a worried glance toward her aunt, but was relieved to see that the tension on her face had disappeared as she enjoyed Captain Kendall's storytelling.

Mabel Irving should *never* have said such a

dreadful thing, Tiria thought angrily. As if agreeing with her sentiments, Clayton Burt said softly, "That was a senseless remark."

Startled, Tiria turned. Although they had been introduced at the beginning of dinner, Tiria and her seatmate had not exchanged a single word all evening. From casual conversation, Tiria had learned that Clayton Burt managed the Russell Motor Car Company in Toronto and was crossing to Europe on the *Empress* for a tour of car factories.

"Well, it's what you were thinking, wasn't it?" he demanded in a friendly voice.

Tiria found herself nodding, then the two of them began chatting easily. She found herself opening up to this loud, but likable man. They began talking about everything from her life in New Zealand to their favorite hobbies.

"Swimming is my favorite sport," Tiria exclaimed.

"Mine, too!" Mr. Burt said with a smile.

All too soon the six-course meal was finished. Clayton Burt thanked Tiria for a lively discussion and leaned down to whisper, "Now, you make sure your aunt forgets all about that upsetting premonition nonsense. This ship is as right as rain, and you can stake Clayton Burt's name and reputation on that!"

Tiria smiled, feeling touched by his concern. As

much as she didn't like admitting it, the story of Mabel Irving's maid had planted a tiny seed of fear in her own mind, as well. When the Irvings and their fellow actors invited Aunt Wynnie and Tiria to join them in the music room to listen to piano playing and to play a game of patience, Tiria was secretly relieved when her aunt refused.

"It's been a long day and this child is going to bed," Aunt Wynnie said firmly.

"Aunt Wynn!" Tiria hissed in embarrassment after the other passengers had departed. She was mortified to have been called a child.

"At least let's sit in the library," Tiria pleaded, not wanting the evening to end. "There are so many books I want to look at."

Aunt Wynnie shook her head.

"Then how about a stroll around the lower promenade deck? It's such a lovely night."

When they came out on deck, the night sky was clear, but a brisk chilly wind had picked up.

"No walk for us," Aunt Wynnie declared.

Tiria was about to protest, but gave up after she glimpsed the set expression on her aunt's face. When she got that look, no amount of pleading or cajoling could sway her. Sighing, Tiria followed her aunt back to their staterooms.

The night stewards were knocking at passenger

doors, jingling large brass keys.

"What's going on?" Aunt Wynnie asked when Chief Steward Gaade entered their corridor.

"No cause for alarm," he assured them both. "We make a tour of inspection each night to make sure that the portholes are securely closed and locked. It's simply a safety precaution."

Later, after the steward had closed and locked the two portholes in her private stateroom, Tiria lay in bed, listening to the comforting hum of the engines far below. Dinner had been an exciting—if overly stimulating—experience, she reflected. As much as she had enjoyed the lively conversation of the Irvings, she did *not* like the story of the maid's premonition and dream. It was all just the superstitious ramblings of an uneducated young girl, Tiria told herself. It didn't mean a thing.

But clutching at her blankets, Tiria stared into the darkness for a long, long time before she finally fell asleep.

Rammed!

Inside the tiny wireless room, Ronald was just finishing his six-hour watch. It had been an uneventful night once passengers stopped asking him to send telegrams. There were the usual routine messages transmitted between ships and the big Marconi station at Father Point only a few miles away, but nothing urgent. It was one-thirty in the morning. Tired from sitting for so long, Ronald was more than ready to hand the late-night stretch over to his partner so he could get some rest.

Thrusting aside the curtain that separated the quarters, Ronald called a weary good-night to Eddy, and prepared for bed. Getting into his bunk, Ronald savored the sense of quiet that dropped over the ship at this late hour. Most of the passengers were asleep in their cabins, and the only sounds Ronald heard now were the muted comings and goings of the night crew and the occasional splash of another vessel gliding upstream. The steady beat of the engines deep within the liner sounded like a heartbeat to Ronald, regular, rhythmic, and comforting. It signaled "all was well" like no other sound on the ship. Ronald gave a contented sigh.

Without warning the ship's siren exploded. It went through Ronald like an electric shock. Biting back a startled exclamation, he jumped up to peer out the left-hand window in the room. What was going on? The night was dark and a belt of heavy fog obscured his vision.

Fog! he thought with a twinge of alarm. Just like Chief Officer Steede talked about earlier.

"Oh, dear God!" he heard Eddy cry.

Ronald jerked around. "Eddy, what is it?"

Seconds later he felt a jolt. It was a mild jolt, but Ronald knew that the high location of their quarters on the ship would cushion any impact. Still, the fact that there was very little noise and no sensation of crashing or tearing was a good sign.

"Ronald, get in here!" Eddy demanded in a shaky voice.

Ronald rushed over to join his partner, who was staring in horror out the window.

"Here she is!" Eddy shouted, pointing to something in the darkness. "We got rammed by a ship! She just glided by."

Rammed! he thought. Ronald stared at his junior partner in horrified disbelief. But years of discipline and training at the Marconi Company took over. Ronald jumped into the seat and put on the headphones.

"Eddy, bring me some clothes, as quick as you can."

Reaching for the transmitter key, Ronald felt the adrenaline pump through his body. As first wireless operator, he was now taking command of the situation. Whatever happened in the next crucial minutes or hours, he would be solely and completely responsible for his actions, as well as those of his junior partner.

"Send an SOS!" Eddy blurted when he returned with Ronald's clothes.

But Ronald shook his head. "We can't without direct instructions from the bridge, Eddy. You know the Marconi Company could dismiss us for taking action on our own."

Eddy's face grew pale. "But we could sink if we delay!"

"Stay calm," Ronald said crisply. "I know what to do."

Reaching for the transmitter key, he tapped out the vital "stand by" message to all wireless stations nearby. "Stand by for distress call," read his message. "We have hit something."

Then Ronald waited.

Bad Decision

The wail of a siren woke Tiria from a deep sleep. Confused and dazed, she sat up with a jerk. It was dark in her room. Her stomach tightened into an anxious knot and her heart began racing.

Jumping out of bed in one swift motion, she hurried over to the porthole. Was this a lifeboat drill? she wondered. Erna Kent had told them that the crew performed a number of drills for safety reasons. Perhaps the passengers were required to participate in one, as well. Gazing out the porthole, however, Tiria could see nothing in the darkness except a long, low bank of fog that spread lazily across the gleaming water.

It couldn't be anything serious, she decided, because no stewards were knocking on doors and instructing passengers to put on life jackets. And Officer Gaade had assured them earlier that the water was calm and the skies were clear.

Still, fog *was* blanketing the river, and whistles had begun blowing in addition to the squall of the siren. Better to get dressed and be prepared, even if it turned out to be a drill, as she suspected, or a false alarm. Flicking on the overhead light, Tiria fumbled through the clothes in the upright trunk and hastily pulled out her warmest wool dress. It would be cold out on deck, she decided, even if they remained there for ten minutes or less before being dismissed. "It's an adventure," she told herself as she got dressed. "Something to tell my brothers about when I get home."

Taking long, slow breaths, she pulled out her sturdiest pair of shoes and methodically laced the ties all the way up. Remembering the chill on the promenade deck earlier that evening, she slipped her arms into a heavy overcoat. There, all ready now, and not a moment to lose. The urgency of the siren was beginning to rattle her determination to stay calm and collected.

Tiria stepped out into the deserted hallway and was halfway to the main promenade stairs before she realized she had forgotten to take her life belt. She knew exactly where it was. The cork jacket was folded neatly in a cupboard above the bed. It would only take a matter of seconds to get it. But the corridor was still empty and there were no signs of any trouble or disturbance on board the ship. It's just a drill, Tiria assured herself. Of course I won't need it. She marched down the corridor, away from the stateroom.

I'll go up on deck first to find out the reason for the siren and the whistles, then come back down and join Aunt Wynnie. No sense in both of them having to endure the cold night air. But before she reached the end of the corridor, doors were being flung open. Fellow passengers poured out of their staterooms, some still in pajamas or nightgowns, others completely dressed, like Tiria.

"What's happening?" an elderly gentleman in a robe demanded of a steward rushing by.

"Nothing, it's only a trifle," the steward assured the man, before hurrying past.

Tiria blew out a sigh of relief as she joined the others heading for the stairs to the deck. She had been correct all along. This was simply a false alarm. They would get up on deck and be told to return to their rooms, with sincere apologies for disturbing their sleep.

But the first sign that something was terribly wrong came moments later. A night watchman burst into the crowded corridor and began to light a collection of oil lamps that he placed on the floor at intervals.

"What are you bothering to do that for?" a passenger standing next to Tiria demanded. "We've got electric lights all along the ship."

The night watchman barely glanced up before refocusing on his task. "These are emergency lamps," he said shortly.

"You mean the electricity might . . . *fail*?" the man said in a shocked voice. "We'll be in the dark?"

"Nothing to worry about," the night watchman offered and hurried down the hall.

"Nothing to worry about?" the man repeated angrily. He raised his voice. "He's lying! They're all lying on this blasted ship!"

Calm, stay calm! Tiria commanded herself. Keep your wits about you, and everything will be all right. But her hands were trembling, almost as if they belonged to someone else. She had no control over their shaking, no control over the thudding of her heart.

Tiria was almost to the promenade stairs when the ship gave an alarming lurch. People cried out and clutched at each other as the liner seemed to rear up in the air.

The door to the stateroom on her right flew open, banging into the man who stood directly behind it. Tiria heard a startled cry as Laurence Irving stumbled into the hallway, his face bloodied from the collision. Mabel Irving hurried out of the stateroom and frantically flung her arms around her wounded husband.

"Keep cool," Irving tersely ordered his wife.

As she continued to cling to him, sobbing, Irving forced a life jacket over her head and pushed her along the corridor.

"We'll be fine, old girl," the actor murmured, and then they were lost in the crowd.

Tiria fought a wave of panic brought on by the sight of blood and the raised voices of the other passengers.

Aunt Wynnie, Tiria thought in distress. I've got to go back to help Aunt Wynnie.

But it was too late. The passage was blocked by hysterical people who were pushing forward to the stairs. To add to the confusion, stewards began calling out, offering life jackets to those without them. In a panic, the older passengers, children, and women received the few life jackets available.

I'll be fine, Tiria told herself. I just need to get up on deck. And Aunt Wynnie will probably join me there. Nothing bad is going to happen to me. *To any of us.*

Gritting her teeth, she clutched the corridor walls for support as she made her way to the stairs. Once there, however, she stopped and stared in startled disbelief, just like everyone else. The first-class promenade stairwell fanned out with curving handrails at either side. The *Empress of Ireland* was listing at such a dramatic angle that the stairs rose vertically in the air like a pole. There was no way anyone could climb them.

"What are we going to do?" an older woman cried.

Tiria thought quickly, then leaned down to tuck her long skirt into the edges of her high lace-up shoes.

"We're going to shinny up the rail," she declared.

Taking a deep breath, she grabbed on to the curved wood railing and began to inch her way up.

The Lights Go Out!

In the wireless room Ronald was fighting to stay calm. Fully dressed now, he sat at his station and agonized as seconds ticked by without further word. Three minutes had already passed since he had sent out the "stand by for distress call" message. That had prompted an immediate and reassuring response from the Marconi station at Father Point, only a few miles away.

"Okay," an operator had replied. "Here we are."

Funny how four simple words could relieve so much tension. Ronald hadn't realized he had been holding his breath until Father Point made contact. Even Eddy had managed to rein in his panic when transmission had been made.

But now the ship had begun to list. There was no doubt that the *Empress of Ireland* had sustained serious damage. And there was still no word from the bridge.

"Ronald, you've *got* to send an SOS!" Eddy demanded with a catch in his throat. His face was so stark-white that Ronald could see a smattering of freckles he had never noticed before.

"You want us to lose our jobs?" Ronald retorted. His voice was sharper, harsher than he intended, but the strain was telling on him. It was telling on them both. "Without direct instruction from the bridge we can't send that message."

Suddenly the door burst open. Steede, the chief officer, ashen-faced and in his pajamas, rapped out a command.

"Get off an SOS. The ship is sinking."

Exchanging tense yet relieved glances with his partner, Ronald pulled himself together. Slowly, with more emphasis than usual, he tapped out: "SOS, we have hit something, sinking fast, send help."

Impatient at the extra-long time Ronald was taking to send this crucial message, Eddy lost his temper. "Why aren't you sending at top speed?" he demanded angrily.

Ronald didn't take his eyes off the task at hand. "At this hour of night there aren't any senior operators on watch," he said in measured tones. "I *have* to send it slowly to give the junior operators a chance to understand."

"You're right! I apologize."

Ronald returned to the wireless key, one foot on the deck, the other propped on the bulkhead to keep himself from toppling over. The ship shuddered and seemed to roll another foot on its side.

A reply from Father Point crackled through Ronald's headphones. The operator wanted to know the ocean liner's position so it could send help. Unfortunately, Ronald didn't know. No one from the bridge had come to tell him, and he couldn't leave his post to go and ask. But he remembered that the *Empress* had dropped her pilot at Father Point about thirty minutes before. Doing some quick mental arithmetic and figuring out the ship's approximate speed, Ronald estimated the location of the *Empress*, give or take several miles. He sent off the estimate to Father Point.

Then came another interminable wait. Ronald looked down to find his fingers gripping the wireless key so tightly his knuckles were white. "Breathe, for God's sake," he instructed himself. "Everything will turn out fine."

But then he realized something.

"Eddy, the transmitter's dying!" Ronald said in a low voice.

His heart gave a lurch as he realized what this meant. But he knew his last message had gotten through, because an immediate response from

Father Point crackled in his ear: "Okay, sending *Eureka*, *Lady Evelyn* to your assistance."

Ronald let out a pent-up breath. "Two ships are on their way."

"But will they get here in time?" Edward said tensely. "It could take them almost forty-five minutes or an hour to reach us. And we're in bad shape."

As if to underscore his words, the ship shuddered yet again, and rolled even more dramatically on its side. Pencils, pads, and manuals went crashing to the floor. The power supply failed. The wireless went dead and all the lights went out.

Sink or Swim!

There was noise and chaos when Tiria finally managed to push her way onto the crowded deck. Although the night sky was clear, the river was enshrouded in the same white blanket of fog she had glimpsed earlier. A cold wind blew in off the water, slicing through Tiria's collar and chilling her in a matter of seconds. Luckily for her she was wearing layers of warm clothes. Too many other unfortunate passengers were not. Many of the men still wore the pajamas they had been sleeping in, and the women wore thin nightgowns. Most had no shoes, not even the comfort of slippers.

The din on the boat deck grew increasingly loud as people shouted and pushed to get to lifeboats. Some roughly grabbed at crew members as they hurried by.

"Where are the life jackets?" a stunned-looking man in full evening attire demanded of a sailor.

"We don't know," the sailor confessed before rushing away.

The ship tilted dangerously. With a quick, startled movement Tiria clutched the left-hand rail on the deck as the *Empress* rolled even further on its side. The liner was listing at nearly a forty-five-degree angle to the Saint Lawrence. Others joined her, screaming in panic as they fought to keep from toppling over. Shivering from the cold and shock, Tiria clenched her teeth tightly together.

Oh, God, please help us, please help us all, she silently prayed.

How much longer could she—could *any* of these passengers—hold on? Air hissed from the portholes, and Tiria could make out a loud roaring sound that seemed to come from the area of the boiler room. Time was running out and she had not seen her aunt.

"Aunt Wynnie!" she shouted, craning her head to search the crowded deck. "Aunt Wynnie, are you here?"

Frantically she gazed around, calling her aunt's name over and over, struggling to maintain a grip on the now crowded railing. Passengers holding on next to her were tiring. The ship's deck was sliding almost straight up in the air. As Tiria watched in horror, people were tumbling off the deck into the icy black water below. To add to the nightmarish scene, lifeboats broke apart from their rope moorings and crashed onto the helpless bodies of those already in the water.

And then the Irvings rushed out on deck. Tiria glimpsed the couple as they half slid, half crawled over to the boat deck. To her amazement she watched Laurence Irving struggling to help his wife climb over the railing, and then drop over the side himself. There was a brief splash, a hoarse cry, and then nothing. Will I end up like them? she thought in horror. No, I won't let it happen. I'll keep fighting.

Yet her shoulders were aching from the tension of clinging to the rail. Her hands were becoming slippery with sweat and the moisture from the river. I can't hold on much longer, Tiria thought in panic. The ship gave a hard, wrenching shudder, then rolled completely over. Tiria screamed as the deck vanished beneath her feet and she went down into the sea.

Black frigid water wrapped itself completely around her. It was cold down here, cold and deathly silent. When she tried to lift her arms, the weight of the water acted as an anchor, imprisoning her. Terrified, Tiria thrashed wildly, propelling herself back to the surface. She came up exhausted from the effort, choking on water. The added weight of her soggy coat kept dragging her down. With no life jacket to help her stay afloat, Tiria realized, she wouldn't be able to swim to any of the few lifeboats that seemed an impossible distance away.

Keep your head, she commanded herself. You're Tiria Townshend of Blenheim, New Zealand, and you never give up.

Three men in life jackets came splashing by.

"Help!" Tiria shouted. She stretched out a hand.

The men pushed her away without a word and half kicked, half swam out of reach.

"Look out!" someone hoarsely shouted. "The ship's going down!"

In a hysterical frenzy, screaming passengers spun and twisted in the water, frantically moving away as the *Empress* gave one last convulsive shudder and then disappeared into the inky blackness. People too near the vortex were immediately sucked into the lethal whirlpool. Huge waves crashed over the helpless victims' heads and held them under. Many of those close to her never resurfaced.

Unable to stop herself, Tiria found herself screaming with the others as she was picked up like a rag doll and tossed into the whirlpool. She came up coughing, wiping strands of hair out of her eyes and mouth.

If someone doesn't help me, she realized, I'm going to die.

To her shock and alarm she discovered she no longer felt the cold of the water. She was only frighteningly aware of the numbness seeping through her skin, making her arms and legs feel as if they weren't connected to her body. Another few minutes and she didn't know whether she could control the movement of her limbs. Her feet were completely dead. Her lungs ached and burned from the constant motion of kicking and thrashing to stay afloat. I don't know how much longer I can keep it up, Tiria realized in horror.

A wave crashed over her face. She choked and sputtered, panic making her flail clumsily to keep above water. Then the body of a lifeless passenger bumped into her in the dark and she gasped in revulsion.

It was a nightmare. Everything around her was unreal and twisted and grotesque—from the unconscious or dead survivors floating past, the cries and pleas of others in the water, the sight of the wreckage of the *Empress of Ireland* bobbling along in a wash of deck chairs, suitcases, pieces of clothing, and even a doll. At that very moment, a man splashed toward her in the darkness. He was wearing a life jacket, and gripping on to a large, buoyant suitcase that floated along beside him.

"Help," Tiria barely managed to gasp. "Can you help me?"

Without hesitating, the man pushed the suitcase across. Tiria's arms and hands were nearly frozen, but she clung to the makeshift life preserver with fierce determination. Her soggy overcoat, however, kept dragging her down into the water.

"You need to get that coat off," the stranger said.

There was something familiar about his voice, Tiria thought. It was only when he got close enough to start tugging at her sleeves, that Tiria recognized the kindly stranger as Clayton Burt, her dining companion of five hours before. Her eyes filled with relieved tears at finding a friend in such a terrible time.

"Mr. Burt!" she exclaimed, half laughing, half crying. "Do you remember me? I'm Tiria Townshend."

The burly factory manager stared at her bedraggled face in the darkness, and then gave a short laugh. "We meet again," he said, pausing for breath. "Our swimming skills must help us now."

It took many minutes and considerable effort but Clayton Burt finally peeled off Tiria's water-soaked coat. But the lace-up shoes that also added unwanted weight could not be pried off.

"They're a terrible tie," Tiria admitted.

"No matter, just keep your grip on the suitcase and paddle as hard as you can," Mr. Burt advised her.

"I don't know how much longer I can go on," Tiria said faintly. Her breath came in agonized gasps and her heart was pounding wildly, out of control. If help was a long way off, perhaps she should let go for a moment and try to conserve her strength. But once she loosened the grip on the suitcase, she immediately went under.

No, NO! a voice in her head shrieked at her. Hold on to the suitcase, girl! HOLD ON!

Clayton Burt yanked her out of the water as she reached blindly for the suitcase.

"What are you thinking?" he shouted angrily. "What are you doing? If you want to live you must keep paddling."

I want to live, Tiria vowed. I need to so I can find Aunt Wynnie once all of this is over. Aunt Wynnie . . . Oh, please, be all right.

Filled with fresh determination, Tiria renewed her efforts to stay afloat. Many agonizing minutes passed. Just when she thought she couldn't kick a minute longer, Mr. Burt exclaimed out loud, "There, not too far from us! A lifeboat!"

"Help Is on the Way"

Ronald remained inside the wireless room with Eddy when the lights went out. After a muffled outburst from Eddy, both young men were temporarily silent in the darkness. Ronald intended to get his emergency transmitter up and running to continue signaling for help. The transmitter was powered by primitive wet cells, but he still had enough strength left to raise Father Point. Frantically he began trying to check the ship's position.

Behind him, Eddy nervously cleared his throat.

"How much time do you think has elapsed since the collision?"

Ronald paused for a moment. "I don't know, Eddy, at least six to seven minutes."

"That much time?" Eddy exclaimed. "Ronald, the *Empress* doesn't have too much longer, then. . . ."

"We're not giving up," Ronald snapped, returning to his key. "Marconi officers never give up."

"But, Ronald—" Eddy began. Someone staggered past the open door, then stopped.

"For God's sake, what are you two still doing here?" a junior officer snapped. "Clear out and get to your lifeboat."

Ronald and Eddy realized they didn't have much time, and scrambled out onto the listing deck. The scene that greeted them was like something out of their worst nightmare. Passengers were clinging to the side of the almost upside-down ship. A multitude of agonized voices, crying and pleading, swallowed one another to form one inhuman howl. The small group of Salvation Army members stood bravely on the deck singing the hymn "God Be with You Till We Meet Again."

Captain Kendall was still at his post of command on the extreme wing of the left-hand flying bridge. To Ronald's horror the flying bridge pointed straight up in the air. The captain was hanging desperately on to the bridge with one hand while shouting instructions through a megaphone to his crew. "Keep your heads, there!" Kendall hoarsely cried. "Don't get excited!"

It was too late for that, Ronald thought in despair. The atmosphere on the deck was one of hysteria and panic.

"Ronald . . ." Eddy said in a small, stricken voice.

He grasped on to the rail as the deck rose beneath their feet.

"It will be okay, Eddy," Ronald said. He hoped he looked, and sounded, far more confident than he felt.

He smiled once in a reassuring manner at his junior partner, then turned to the semihysterical passengers who were desperately clinging to the base of the masts and funnels.

"Rescue ships are on the way!" he shouted. "Two ships have been alerted."

A few fearful faces turned to him with a flash of hope, but the final lurch of the *Empress* flung him and the others into the water. Ronald sank deep into the river. Plunging down into the icy water he opened his eyes, but all he could see was the encompassing blackness surrounding him. He scissor-kicked his legs to bring himself back up to the surface.

The cold moist air felt wonderful as he filled his lungs with oxygen. He thrashed about in the freezing water, cursing the fact that he had neglected to take his life jacket. Minutes later, he cursed his junior partner for urging him to wear his overcoat before they left. The weight of the coat was dragging him down. But there was nothing he could do now.

Ronald paddled furiously in the mist-enclosed water, hoping to bump into a lifeboat. Every so often the lifeless bodies of passengers and fellow crew members floated in front of him. Ronald turned his head away, blinking back tears.

Just when he thought he couldn't summon the energy to paddle any longer, he glimpsed a lifeboat not more than five yards away. Ronald shouted for help.

"Give a hand here," someone called from the lifeboat.

Ronald was so exhausted and frozen that he had to be pulled bodily into the boat. When he collapsed against the back of a seat he discovered that he had lost his trousers. He was too drained to care. At least the coat was still around his battered and wet body.

"You're in luck, mate," one of the sailors assured him. "The *Lady Evelyn* just arrived. You'll be warm and dry in no time."

Ronald hunched miserably in the wet overcoat, his teeth chattering.

"Who . . . sank us?" he barely got out.

"The *Storstad*," the sailor said. "A Norwegian freighter, of all things. Can you believe that?"

Ronald shook his head. History was repeating itself in a cruel joke. Two years before, the *Empress of Britain* had collided with a Norwegian coal transporter and the Norwegian vessel had gone down. Now a Norwegian freighter had struck them and the *Empress of Ireland* had sunk.

The Search

At about the same time that Ronald was being transferred to the *Lady Evelyn*, Tiria and Clayton Burt's lifeboat pulled up to a small black ship called the *Storstad*. The crew members informed them that, incredibly enough, this was the Norwegian freighter that had rammed the *Empress*. In the moonlight, Tiria could make out the horribly crushed and twisted starboard bow.

The crew members secured the lifeboat to the freighter. Tiria swallowed nervously when she realized she'd have to climb a high rope ladder to reach the deck. One thought propelled her forward—Aunt Wynnie might be waiting for her among the rest of the survivors.

I can do it, Tiria told herself as she slowly but determinedly pulled her way up. *I climbed the promenade railing and I can do this.*

Tired and exhausted, she forced herself to think

about only one wet and slippery rung at a time. *And don't look down!* she ordered herself after she accidentally glanced at the dark water waiting below. *I'm not ever going to touch that foul river again*, she swore, and renewed her efforts. At the very top, Norwegian-speaking sailors hauled her onto the deck.

Shaking and in a mild state of shock, Tiria found herself surrounded by a mass of *Empress* survivors. There must have been close to two hundred exhausted and trembling people sitting or leaning along the deck. Several of the *Storstad*'s crew wove among the survivors, handing out blankets and spare clothing, and offering coffee from a large urn.

"There now, coffee's what you need," Clayton Burt commanded, coming to stand behind her.

But Tiria weakly shook her head. "I have to find my aunt."

"You need something warm in you first," Clayton Burt urged. He thrust a steaming cup into Tiria's freezing hands. "Now drink this."

Too exhausted to argue, she sipped at the black liquid.

"Look, Captain Kendall's coming aboard!" someone behind Tiria said.

"Oh, the poor man looks so sick," Tiria exclaimed. "He's got bruises on his face."

"He's had the worst night of his life," Clayton Burt said.

Wearily, the captain climbed to the top of the *Storstad*'s deck and stopped when a burly, thick-necked man with a red face and thick mustache approached him.

"Are you the master of this ship?" Captain Kendall angrily demanded.

"I am," the man said in accented English.

"You have sunk my ship," Kendall accused him. "You were going full speed ahead through dense fog."

"I was *not* going full speed," the Norwegian captain answered. "You were going full speed."

The two men bristled at each other like dogs ready to attack, Tiria thought. Any minute fists would start flying.

An authoritative-looking man in uniform got between the two warring captains and held them apart.

"Don't say anything," the man instructed Captain Kendall. "You'd better go below."

Scowling in fury but managing to restrain himself, the captain of the *Empress* spun on his heel and went into the chart room.

"Mercy," Tiria whispered.

"There's bound to be a thorough investigation of tonight's collision," Clayton Burt said softly. "The two captains cannot both be right."

Tiria didn't care about that. Her only concern was

locating her aunt. Finishing her coffee, she began to circulate around the crowded decks, peering hopefully into faces and calling her aunt's name. Clayton Burt remained at her side, keeping her spirits up. Yet each time they found someone who resembled her aunt from a distance, then discovered it was not, Tiria's hopes sank. When they found no trace of Aunt Wynnie on the top deck, Tiria's face crumpled.

"Oh, no, she's not here!" she whispered, clutching at Clayton Burt's sleeve. "She's not here!"

"She may be below," he suggested. "Many of the rescued passengers are probably in the engine or boiler rooms, trying to get warm."

Clinging to a shred of hope, Tiria followed the factory manager below deck. They bumped into *Empress* survivors wearing chenille drapes, newspapers, and in one case, a single pillowcase. They passed crew bunks occupied by shivering passengers huddled together. They walked by a makeshift operating room where a young doctor was examining the more seriously wounded and setting splints for broken bones. In every bunk, in every quarter or room, Tiria examined faces for the one she desperately wanted to see.

"Aunt Wynnie, please let me find you," she whispered, her fear giving way to dread. "Please be on this ship."

There was only one area she hadn't searched, and that was the engine room.

Tiria and Clayton Burt came through the door of the engine room, but abruptly stopped. Over a hundred or more survivors crowded into this noisy, blazingly hot space. Some of them leaned against the boiling-hot cylinders, oblivious to the pain. Others huddled on the floor, desperately trying to unthaw. Many were shrieking incoherently in languages Tiria didn't understand. It was like something out of an insane asylum, Tiria thought as she fought back panic. How would she ever hope to find her aunt in this mass of people? Worse yet, what if Aunt Wynnie was *not* here, on board the *Storstad?* What if Aunt Wynnie had never gotten off the *Empress?* No, she couldn't allow herself to think that. Trembling, fearing the worst, Tiria felt Mr. Burt's hand on her shoulder.

"Would you like some help?" he said.

She couldn't get the words out. She could only nod silently, thankful for his compassion and help at the worst moment of her life. As if sensing her feelings, Mr. Burt didn't demand a response.

"Whatever happens," he said softly, but with conviction, "you'll be able to face it. Look at the courage you displayed tonight. You're a survivor, Tiria. You kept going when others would have given up."

Was she? Tiria thought. She hadn't thought of herself as being particularly courageous or brave, just determined to keep going at any cost. She would keep going now, not only for her aunt's sake, but her own, as well.

"I'm ready to start looking for Aunt Wynnie," she said. "If you'll help me."

Clayton Burt smiled at her briefly, and they entered the engine room.

The *Lady Evelyn*

Ronald leaned against the railing on the upper deck of the *Lady Evelyn*, taking a moment to rest after being pulled aboard. It was now almost four in the morning and the skies were still dark. All traces of the deadly fog that had caused the fateful collision were gone. The lights shining out of the *Lady Evelyn*'s portholes revealed a tranquil, calm river.

Ronald angrily curled his hands into fists. Why hadn't the weather stayed clear? Why had that infernal fog sprung up and caused the two ships to crash into each other?

What was the sense of going over that now? he thought. There had been a number of survivors and many of his crew mates from the *Empress of Ireland* had been picked up and brought to this steamer, as well as a small band of passengers. After talking to the officers of the ship, Ronald had learned that the *Lady Evelyn* had sped into the night just two minutes after receiving the SOS call. She had sailed blindly through dense fog at full speed to reach the liner, taking dangerous risks. The steamer arrived at the scene of the disaster nearly fifty minutes later, but by then it was too late. The *Empress* had gone under and there were few people alive in the river.

Ronald's lips had tightened when he heard this account. Could he have done something else—anything at all—to have helped or saved more lives tonight? It wasn't too late, even now. Although he was bone tired, nearly frozen, and in a daze, Ronald realized there was work to be done. Stopping one of the ship's crew, he asked if there was a wireless aboard.

The sailor frowned. "The ship just installed a wireless, but there's no operator, I fear. The captain didn't have time to hire one yet, so that won't be much good to you."

"Better than you think," Ronald replied, feeling his energy return. "I was the senior operator on the *Empress of Ireland*. Could you direct me to the wireless room?"

Eager to be helpful, the sailor led Ronald along passageways until they came to the bridge and the officers' quarters.

"The wireless is in here," the sailor said, indicating a small room.

Ronald tried the door, but found it locked. He gave it an angry kick.

"I don't believe the bad luck of this evening," Ronald sputtered impatiently. "Well, a locked door won't stop me from my work."

"What are you planning to do?" the sailor said.

"I'm going to break the door down," Ronald replied. "And you're going to help me."

"No, I can't," the young man said, swallowing nervously.

"Then I'll do it myself," Ronald declared. "I'll take full responsibility with your captain. In fact, you can report to him and inform him that the *Lady Evelyn* is now equipped to take and send wireless transmissions. Tell him that Ronald Ferguson of the Marconi Company is in command."

Once Ronald was alone, he took a deep breath. As weak as he was, the need to send messages for medical supplies and clothing for the survivors gave him added strength. With one great shove, he forced the door open and promptly sat down in front of the wireless keys. It felt good to be taking action again. With ease and increasing speed, Ronald began transmitting to Father Point.

It had been a long, traumatic night, but dawn was finally breaking when Ronald finished. His wrists ached, as did his entire body from sitting in one spot for so long. And his stomach was rumbling from hunger. The last time he had eaten anything was at dinner more than eleven hours before.

Taking a deep breath, he removed the head-phones and stood up. He stretched for a moment, then went out on deck. It was cold this morning, below forty degrees, he estimated. He shivered and shoved his hands into the pockets of his overcoat. Despite the chilly conditions, the crew had been busy. While Ronald had been transmitting all those hours, the men of the *Lady Evelyn* had been arranging the dead bodies inside rough-hewn wooden coffins. Row upon row of coffins stretched out in ragged lines up and down the deck. There were so many coffins, Ronald thought. So many lives lost.

Ronald leaned tiredly against the railing, sad-dened by the sight. Then he glanced across the river and realized the steamer was slowly pulling into the quay at Rimouski Wharf. Rimouski, a little riverside port, was two hundred miles from the *Empress of Ireland*'s original point of departure. It would be here that the shocked and wounded passengers (as well as the dead) would be dropped off for special trains taking them back to Quebec. Already the sixty or more survivors had come out on deck and were hud-dling together anxiously in the cold.

Some of them were nearly naked. Others were

barely covered by scraps of clothing, blankets, sheets, or pillowcases. Many were wounded, with sprains, fractured or broken bones and were suffering from the devastating effects of prolonged exposure to the freezing river. Ronald could hear their moans and cries from his position on the officers' deck.

Where were the medical supplies, food, and clothing he had requested? He had been transmitting pleas for these necessities all night. Had it all been in vain?

A shout suddenly went up. Officers of the steamer began pointing to something in the distance. Some of the more able passengers staggered to their feet and uttered weak cries of relieved joy.

Ronald squinted into the horizon. His heart leaped. Horse-drawn wagons and carts were heading toward the quay over cobblestones and mud. He counted three, four, no five carts and wagons in all. When they pulled up dockside to the *Lady Evelyn*, a uniformed officer gave them instructions where to wait.

"We have food and coffee," one of the drivers shouted. "We brought bandages, splints, and other medical supplies."

A great cheer rose from everyone aboard the steamer.

"What about clothing?" a barely covered passenger called, shivering miserably in the morning chill.

"There's plenty of that," another helper responded. "And blankets to warm you. Our doctors are standing by to help the seriously injured."

"Thank God," one of the survivors said softly.

"Thank God," many repeated.

A few burst into grateful tears as they disembarked and were shepherded into the comforting hands of those on the dock. Ronald remained on the officers' deck, watching in silence as the survivors received aid. Although he was not completely or properly dressed in uniform, he had never felt more proud—or more rewarded—to serve the Marconi Company than he did at this moment. Nothing could bring back the lives of those lost at sea, but his efforts would go a long way in helping those survive the ordeal.

As the sun burned off the morning chill, Ronald made his way to the captain's quarters. He turned his face to the warming rays and smiled.

Epilogue

News of the sinking of the *Empress of Ireland* brought shock waves to English-speaking countries around the world. "Another *Titanic* Disaster!" one British headline read. Of the 1,477 who sailed that fateful night, 1,012 lost their lives, including 840 passengers, eight more than had died on board the *Titanic*.

It was a maritime disaster of the worst kind, but it was also a mystery. The questions of why and how a small Norwegian freighter collided with a massive ocean liner in a body of water more than thirty miles wide remain unanswered to this day. The Saint Lawrence provided more than enough space for two ships to pass each other in safety. Both of the ships had navigation lights (blinking green on the right, red on the left) that should have alerted navigators on both bridges to each other's presence, even in dense fog.

At a public inquiry, the captain of the *Empress of Ireland* and the captain of the *Storstad* each swore that the other ship had abruptly changed course in heavy fog without any warning. No evidence could be produced proving either man right. In the end, experts decided that although the fog was to blame for the tragedy, there had been more negligence on board the *Storstad*.

There is no mystery, however, as to why and how an ocean liner, second in size only to the *Titanic* at that time, sank in just fourteen minutes. The *Storstad*'s reinforced steel bow sliced into the *Empress of Ireland*'s unprotected side like a warm knife into butter. The hole in the *Empress* was estimated to be 25 feet high by 14 feet wide, or about 350 square feet. The waters of the Saint Lawrence swept into the fatal opening at a rate of 60,000 gallons per second.

Also, a number of portholes had been left open that evening for several of the passengers to enjoy the evening air. Once the great liner began to list starboard, water began gushing into the open portholes. Within seconds, a tidal wave crashed and spread through the lower decks, drowning the passengers asleep in their beds. After ten minutes of taking on water, the ocean liner lurched onto her side with hundreds of passengers clinging to her hull. Four minutes later she gave a final sharp tilt and sank to the bottom of the river.

Over 80 percent of the passengers died that night. The famous stage couple who had entertained Tiria and Aunt Wynnie at dinner, Laurence and Mabel Irving, drowned, but only Laurence Irving's body was properly identified, by his ring. Their friends in the acting troupe, the Nevilles, also died, along with Mabel Irving's maid, Hilda Hagerson.

To her shock and great sorrow, Tiria Townshend learned that her aunt had not been picked up by either of the rescue ships. Late in the morning of May 30, Tiria had to file past row upon row of open coffins at the dock in Quebec, searching for her aunt. Exposure to the water caused bloating and disfigurement in the drowning victims. When Tiria finally pointed to the coffin that contained her aunt's body, surviving crew members stepped in to contest her identification. "That is the body of our friend and fellow stewardess, Mrs. Leader," they insisted. It was only after Tiria revealed a small mark on her aunt's body that she finally won her claim. Seventeen-year-old Tiria Townshend returned to New Zealand with a casket and memories of a tragic night she would never forget.

Her fellow passenger and helpful companion, Clayton Burt, eagerly returned to Indiana to join his wife and family. But he, too, held on to his own memories of that fateful crossing and the young woman who shared the most terrifying night of his life.

Both Ronald Ferguson and Edward Bamford were interviewed at the public investigation. At the end of their accounts of the sinking, the chairman of the inquiry, John Charles Bigham, made a point of commending them for remaining in the wireless room until the very end, and singled out Ronald Ferguson for special praise for continuing to send for help on board the *Lady Evelyn*. "You young gentlemen," John Bigham said, "did great credit to the service you are in."

Ronald Ferguson spent the rest of his life in the work he loved so well, that of radio. Following war service in the Royal Flying Corps, he was employed by the Radio Communication Company, the precursor to England's BBC (British Broadcasting Company). In 1927 he returned to marine radio with the British Wireless Marine Service and later as General Manager of Marconi International Marine. In 1961 he retired from Marconi International Marine, but served as a member of its board of directors for several years following.

In 1980 famed oceanographer Jacques Cousteau and his son explored the Saint Lawrence seaway in his vessel, *Calypso*. The purpose of the underwater exploration was to locate the buried wreck of the *Empress of Ireland*. Many distinguished passengers accompanied Cousteau and his son on this televised voyage, none more distinguished, however, than eighty-four-year-old Ronald Ferguson. The one-time *Empress* wireless operator was able to point out the whereabouts of the small deckhouse for the *Calypso* crew once they had found the ship, and to recount in detail the events of that dramatic night.

Seven years later Ronald Ferguson died at the age of ninety-one.

He was one of England's quiet heroes.

Arctic Crash

The crash of the airship Italia
and the rescue of its survivors,

May 25–July 12, 1928

In 1928, airships—not airplanes—ruled the skies. The six-hundred-foot-long dirigibles floated overhead like silvery ghosts. They were the only craft strong enough to withstand the high winds and storms that frequently occurred during transatlantic crossings.

One of the best-known designers and manufacturers of airships was General Umberto Nobile. Ever since Swedish aviator Salomon Andrée's fatal polar crossing by balloon in 1897, Italy and Norway had wanted to conquer the North Pole by dirigible. In 1926, Norwegian explorer Roald Amundsen hired Italian airship commander Nobile to attempt the first crossing of the North Pole in the *Norge*. The expedition proved successful, although relations were strained between the two countries over who deserved credit for the flight. Nobile went on to create his own semirigid dirigible, *Italia*, to return to the North Pole for scientific exploration and the search for new land. On May 23, 1928, Nobile and an experienced crew of sixteen men lifted off from Milan, Italy, on what they hoped would be a historic journey.

All too soon, however, Nobile's polar dream turned into a nightmare. The *Italia* encountered gale-force winds and fog on May 25, 1928, and the control cabin crashed into an ice pack in the Arctic Ocean. Nine men and one dog found themselves marooned in an isolated wasteland, but they never gave up hope and the will to live, in one of the most exciting yet tragic air disasters of the era.

Lifting Off

He hadn't been chosen.

Alfredo Viglieri's heart sank when he saw his bag of personal gear and clothing being taken out of the cabin of the airship. There had always been a question as to whether the *Italia* could carry an extra navigation officer, and now the twenty-eight-year-old Royal Naval lieutenant had gotten his answer. He would have to remain behind while the other fifteen lucky crew members and officers got to fly on this historic expedition to the North Pole on May 23, 1928. General Umberto Nobile, the designer of the *Italia*, a 348-foot-long semirigid dirigible, was its commander. He had told the men that their purpose in flying over the largely unexplored ice cap was to make an aerial survey of the deserted stretch of ice and snow near Greenland and to touch down at the North Pole for scientific examination.

"It's been a race to the Pole for almost sixty

years," Nobile had explained, "and only Admiral Byrd has claimed to fly over it by plane. But three years ago explorer Roald Amundsen from Sweden and Lincoln Ellsworth from America hired me to fly my dirigible, the *Norge*, on a joint polar expedition that ultimately crossed the Pole. Some of you were on that flight with me and know we didn't discover any new land and were unable to get close because of bad weather. But this time I feel confident we will make history by landing at the Pole itself."

Alfredo and his fellow officers had been inspired by Nobile's enthusiasm and determination to be the first to conquer the Pole. Not one considered backing out of the potentially dangerous expedition. Now Alfredo stared up at the massive dirigible in its roofless hangar. Although it was four o'clock in the morning, brilliant sunshine lit up the cold, frozen dawn at Spitzbergen, a Norwegian outpost. Alfredo shivered, glancing across at the snow-covered mountains and the glittering expanse of ice. He still couldn't get over the fact that the tip of the Arctic islands enjoyed twenty-four hours of daylight during late spring and early summer, although rising winds could sometimes cause problems with a dirigible launch. The air was extremely calm today, so the *Italia* would lift off easily.

"I should be going," Alfredo murmured under

his breath. He stared glumly at the lucky crew members boarding the dirigible.

"Good news!" someone cried behind him. "I've been cleared for the expedition!"

Alfredo turned to find Francis Behounek beaming from ear to ear. The Czechoslovakian scientist couldn't contain his excitement. Alfredo had gotten to know the soft-spoken but big and bulky thirty-one-year-old professor on the trial flight from Milan.

"Congratulations," Alfredo said with an envious smile. He shook the professor's hand and watched him lumber over to the hangar. There wasn't much time now. Alfredo had just learned that weather reports predicted increasing fog and mist along the coast. The general would want to take advantage of the sunshine and clear skies to lift off soon.

The engines of the massive airship were already running, ticking over slowly. The one hundred and fifty men of the ground crew grabbed on to the mooring ropes that held the buoyant airship just above the ground. A priest stood beside the men, waiting for the moment when he'd say the final prayers. Alfredo searched the length of the dirigible for sight of the general, and found him. Nobile was moving from group to group, checking on the final loading preparations, motioning for Cecioni, the motor mechanic, to finish testing the engines.

Titina, Nobile's playful pet terrier, followed at her master's heels. It may have seemed silly or odd to some, but the general always insisted on bringing Titina along with him on his flights. And this flight to the Pole was no exception.

Only a few more minutes, Alfredo thought, and the general would give the word. Alfredo stood there with a smile on his face, but inside he was panicking as the airship was pulled out onto the ice-covered field. Just at that moment, General Nobile jumped out of the control cabin and seemed to motion to him. Alfredo's heart gave a sudden, hopeful lurch.

"You want to talk to me, General?" he yelled above the throb of the engines.

Nobile's normally composed face broke into an unexpected grin.

"Hurry up and get on board!" the general commanded.

Alfredo stood there for one shocked moment, then saluted sharply. He hurried over to pick up his bag of clothing and gear, then hopped on board the control cabin, followed by Nobile. There were smiles all around from his fellow officers, as Alfredo deposited his belongings in the gangway and then went to take up his post at the navigation table at the rear of the cabin. He was so excited that he barely heard the softly murmured prayer of Father

Franceschi on the ground directly below.

There was a minute of silence among the men after the priest gave the final blessing, then Nobile ordered, "Let go!"

Titina yapped as if she sensed the importance of the dramatic moment.

The ground crew released their hold on the mooring ropes. When the ropes slipped off, the men roared out cheers and best wishes. The three engines on the airship speeded up into a thunderous noise.

Alfredo watched from the control window as the *Italia* lifted into the frigid sky, and headed for the entrance to King's Bay and then on to the Pole. He couldn't believe his luck. A delicious feeling of adventure swept over him. Just like my hero, Lucky Lindy, I'm getting my own chance to fly, Alfredo thought. This was one voyage he would never forget, he realized, and if it turned out the way General Nobile expected, it would be a voyage for the history books.

Storm Warnings!

Francis Behounek was adjusting a meteorological instrument in the control cabin a little past midnight when someone cried, "We're here!" The Czech scientist spun around to see First Officer Mariano point to his sextant with a triumphant smile. All of the officers immediately stopped talking.

Francis didn't need to ask anyone what that simple phrase meant: the Pole had been sighted. Francis knew that many explorers had lost their lives attempting to reach this desolate spot. If all went as planned for the *Italia*, however, General Nobile would claim the honors of being the first man to cross and then land at the Pole. And Italy would be recognized as the first country to conquer the mysterious Arctic.

"I hope General Nobile experiences better luck this time around," someone murmured behind him.

Startled, Francis turned to find Finn Malmgren,

the second meteorologist on the expedition, calmly gazing out the window.

"What do you mean, *this* time?" Francis said.

Malmgren, a thirty-year-old Swedish professor, was the only other non-Italian on board the dirigible, and the two men shared a friendly bond because of this distinction.

"Weren't you told about Nobile's very first dirigible, the *Roma*?" Malmgren asked.

Francis shook his head.

"The *Roma* was sold to America in 1920, but she didn't fare very well on her first flight over Virginia two years later."

Francis swallowed nervously. "Why, what happened?"

Malmgren gravely shook his head. "The dirigible exploded midair and thirty-two men were killed. So let's both hope that the general's luck holds out on *this* flight."

"Do you really believe that anything—*bad* can happen to us?" Francis asked thoughtfully.

"I don't think so," Malmgren replied. "General Nobile's first-rate as an aircraft commander and this time he's got it right."

"All engines, half speed," General Nobile shouted to Chief Engineer Ettore Arduino. "Helm full circle. Elevators down."

The *Italia* eased through the clouds and mist until all the men on board could see the ice pack clearly. Francis thought about the comments that Malmgren had made. What if a disaster were to happen to the airship? Granted, he was wearing woollen underwear, long woollen socks, solid leather shoes, and a thick woollen suit, topped with another lambskin covering with a hood. All the men were. And General Nobile insisted that each man be equipped with a good watch, a pocket compass, and two pairs of dark glasses for protection against snow blindness. The heavy outer clothing would help them withstand temperatures as low as twenty-one degrees below zero and still march along the ice. But for how long? And what if a storm came up when they were conducting experiments out on the ice? Would they be able to return to the safety of the dirigible in the flotation device that had never—to his knowledge—been tested before?

"This is a perfect time to measure the magnetic field," said Professor Aldo Pontremoli, beside him.

The Italian professor of physics from the University of Milan was the third scientist who had been selected for the expedition.

While both men returned to their instruments, music unexpectedly filled the cabin. Francis turned to see that an officer had put a record on the gramophone, a tune Pontremoli told him was the Fascist battle hymn, "Giovinezza."

The Italian officers were celebrating this historic moment. Many of the men were even crying. General Nobile was leaning out of the cabin, clutching the Italian flag, waiting for the perfect spot to drop the tricolor. Titina danced around the general's feet. Even though Nobile had dropped an Italian flag (along with much smaller Norwegian and American flags) at the Pole three years earlier, the moment now was highly charged. Nobile lowered the flag on to the ice pack, followed by a religious medal, and then a large oak cross given to him by Pope Pius XI. The men saluted the objects. Radio operator Guiseppe Biagi sent off a message to Rome, to the pope, to the king, and to Mussolini, announcing the accomplishment.

One by one the senior officers approached the airship commander and saluted him, some crying, "*Viva Nobile!*" Getting into the spirit of the moment, Francis went over and shook the general's hand.

They drank a toast of eggnog specially prepared in Italy and saved for the occasion. Then after two hours circling the Pole, the *Italia* headed south on her return flight—into swirling mists and heavy wind.

Francis peered out the port window with a sinking feeling in his gut. A storm was blocking their path. Now savage winds battered the hydrogen-filled dirigible, and whistled eerily inside the cracks of the canvas-covered cabin. The aircraft twisted and bucked under the force of the dark, heavy clouds.

"It's not so bad," Pontremoli said softly after a particularly bad shudder of the *Italia*. "I've been through worse."

Francis smiled weakly, too nervous to respond, when a crack, like a rifle shot, sounded above the throb of the engines and the whine of the winds.

"Ice!" First Officer Mariano shouted. "It's being flung from the propeller blades. We need to get out of the way of the storm before it's too late!"

Francis turned a worried face to his fellow scientist for reassurance, but Pontremoli looked just as scared as he.

Flying into the Storm

By four-thirty the next morning the situation had worsened. Heavy winds and gusts of icy fog blew the *Italia* from side to side. The fuel supply was dropping at an alarming rate. Alfredo stood by the steering wheel, trying to stay alert. No one had slept during the night as they struggled to keep the airship on course.

"The situation is serious," Alfredo overheard Cecioni remark to the general. "Running on all three engines at the same time has been eating away at our supply of fuel. And we're moving at a crawl against these winds."

"Increase speed and get us out of this storm," Nobile commanded.

Alfredo was bent over the navigation charts when a violent lurch of the cabin made him grab on to the table for support. The gale winds of the ice storm tossed the dirigible around with fury, and hissed through the cracks of the canvas walls of the control cabin. Alfredo shivered as the freezing drafts blew across his face and neck.

"Hold on course!" First Officer Mariano ordered the helmsman, Commander Filippo Zappi.

"Impossible," Zappi retorted. "Every time I fight her onto the proper course we get a blast that turns her tail around."

"He's right," Francis said, coming forward from his post. "I've been making my own compass calculations. Look," he continued, "the ship's off course by as much as thirty degrees."

Zappi had to wrestle with the wheel to keep the *Italia* straight. All the men in the crowded cabin could hear the wrenching of the giant vertical fin as the rudder strained against the wind.

Alfredo frowned. No one could plot a course or track for the airship if the storm's winds made her zigzag violently. That meant transmitting her exact location would be almost impossible, as well. There wasn't even a glimmer of sunlight, so they couldn't get a sextant reading, either. If anything happened to the ship, they'd be cut off.

"Just let us get through this ice storm," Alfredo prayed beneath his breath.

"We're Going Down!"

Francis stretched, then took another sip of coffee. It was nine-thirty in the morning. He was taking a short break while Pontremoli slept on the gangway inside the ship. Francis had stolen a few short hours himself at dawn, but was still feeling the effects of fatigue and constant worry. Peering out the ice-encrusted porthole window, he was relieved to see the airship rising through the clouds and into brilliant sunshine. Perhaps the worst was over.

Rays of the sun streamed into the cabin. Winds still rocked the dirigible, but they were much lighter. With the engines temporarily switched off, the *Italia* rose like a weightless balloon.

"The pressure is going up, General," Alfredo reported.

Francis noted the sudden looks of concern that crossed the faces of the senior officers.

"What's happening?" Francis asked his friend

Malmgren, who stopped beside him. "I don't understand why everyone's so anxious."

"We're in trouble," Malmgren replied softly. "Ice pellets thrown by the propeller have punctured the skin of the aircraft and hydrogen's been released."

"But we're weightless right now," Francis protested. "How could the aircraft be so light if we've lost too much hydrogen gas?"

"That's only because the engines are temporarily stopped to save our fuel," Malmgren explained. "The aircraft will always rise on its own without the engines to propel it forward."

"Quickly, take your measurements and get a bearing of our location," Nobile ordered his navigational officers. "We need to descend without delay."

"Why is the general worried?" Francis whispered to Malmgren.

"Staying too long in the sun could cause the hydrogen gas to expand so much that we'd almost be too light. Then we'd have to valve off such a large quantity of hydrogen in order to descend that we'd become dangerously heavy. If too much hydrogen is released, we'd certainly sink." Malmgren shook his head. "We don't need the loss of hydrogen along with all the ice and snow that's collected on the frame and is weighing us down."

Thirty minutes later the general ordered two of

the three engines started. The *Italia* eased down into the mists. At one thousand feet Francis could catch glimpses of the ice pack below through gaps in the snow and clouds.

The airship cruised without difficulty for the next half hour.

"The head wind has diminished," Nobile informed the officers. "At our present rate of speed we should reach Spitzbergen between three and four o'clock this afternoon."

The worst is over, Francis thought with relief.

But just then Malmgren pulled him to one side.

"I don't think we're going to make it," Malmgren blurted out under his breath. "We're only staying in the air now by using the force of the motors. If we have to shut down the engines for any reason, we'll descend. We've lost too much hydrogen."

Francis worriedly glanced at the altimeter. "But there's no sign we're sinking!"

"I hope I'm wrong," Malmgren said and returned to take over the rudder wheel. Francis glanced over at him, alarm bells going off in his mind. The *Roma*, he thought in horror. Are we going to end up like the *Roma*? Seconds later the chief technician turned from the elevator wheel and shouted, "We're heavy!"

Francis spun around, noting General Nobile's

alarmed expression. Titina had been sleeping in one of the holds, but woke up with playful barks. She scampered over to her master, ready for games or some fun, but the commander ignored her to shout out commands: "All engines. Emergency. Ahead at full!"

"We're going down!" one of the navigational officers announced in a tense voice. "By eight degrees. We're falling at the rate of two feet per second!"

Falling! Francis took a shocked step forward. This couldn't be happening, not when they were so close to home. Perhaps even now, however, Nobile could bring the dirigible up.

But it was too late. The general was preparing the aircraft for a crash landing. Nobile ordered the telegraph to be rung. "Stop all engines!" he commanded. He turned to Cecioni at the elevator wheel. "Release the ballast chain. Break our fall!"

But Francis saw that Cecioni was having trouble unfastening the heavy chains that served as a ladder when the ship was landed. Throwing out this added weight could lighten the dirigible's load and bring her down to land more gently. Francis hurried over to Cecioni, who had fallen to his hands and knees in his panic to unfasten the chains. Together the two men grappled with the weighted chains until they realized it was too late.

Within minutes, possibly seconds, the airship would crash.

Francis scrambled to his feet to peer out the window.

"Look! There's the ice pack!" Malgrem shouted from the nose of the cabin.

The *Italia* was sliding, stern first, to the ice-encrusted wasteland directly below. Three hundred fifty feet of airship, a hull as large as that of a naval destroyer but much lighter and more fragile, rushed down out of the sky in less than three minutes.

Francis gripped the railing of the cabin with a white-knuckled hand and gazed down in horror. The jagged ice pack seemed to be flying up to meet them, hurtling toward the dirigible with nightmare speed.

Instinctively Francis pulled his head away from the glass and closed his eyes.

This is the end, he thought.

Within seconds Francis felt a great shudder run through the ship, followed by a shattering sound. The cabin struck the ice with brutal force, plunged into the snow-covered ice, and split into pieces. Men screamed.

Then all was silent.

"SOS *Italia…*"

Alfredo groaned and opened his eyes. He found himself lying on his back in a tangle of canvas and twisted framework, staring up through the slashed roof of the cabin. Just moments before he had been standing at the navigational chart table with First Officer Mariano. Now he lay tossed down on the ice pack.

The dirigible swayed directly above him. At any moment the weight of the airship could collapse and smother him. Or worse, the hydrogen might catch fire and burn him to death.

But as he scrambled to his feet in panic, Alfredo realized that the body of the airship had broken free from the control cabin. The cabin had been sliced off from the impact on the ice, as well as the engine gondolas. Buoyed by the force of the winds, the dirigible began to rise slowly. With no motors to propel it, the *Italia* was at the mercy of the gale.

And then Alfredo spotted something that made the hairs rise on the back of his neck. Two of the men still on board the aircraft rushed to the gaping hole where the control cabin had been. Pontremoli and Arduino stared down at Alfredo on the ice. They were imprisoned inside a dirigible that they could not control or navigate. No one said a word for several tense moments. Pontremoli fearfully drew back from the torn hole in the canvas, but Arduino went into action, tossing fuel, provisions, and equipment overboard to the crew members on the ice. Then, within a matter of seconds, the hull of the airship rose into the sky and drifted away, gathering speed in the gale winds.

It would never return, Alfredo thought numbly. Without the use of its engines, the airship was doomed, along with the crew still trapped inside.

With a heartsick feeling he turned to survey the wreckage on the ground. It was a nightmare scene, with bodies and pieces of the airship scattered over the jagged peaks of the ice.

But he was a naval officer. He had a job to do. His first priority was to locate General Nobile to see if he was all right and able to take command. Hearing Titina's frenzied barking in the distance, Alfredo followed the sound to her and her master.

Francis felt something heavy pressing down on him from all sides, suffocating him. Cold wet stuff covered his eyes and nose. Panicking, he jerked his hands and legs from out of this hold and shakily got to his feet. He was standing in masses of snow in the middle of an ice storm. The control cabin had shattered into pieces, spilling him violently onto the ice pack, but the remaining body of the dirigible was already floating away.

"Come back!" Francis shouted, but the winds blunted his words.

It didn't matter if they heard, he realized. Without the control cabin to navigate the ship, the aircraft *couldn't* come back.

Francis spun around, trying to see if anyone else had survived the crash. The dog was barking but he couldn't see clearly in the storm.

And then he heard voices.

Men began stirring and getting up.

Francis found Malmgren, alive and standing. But Malmgren's face was twisted in pain.

"My left side's been battered from the crash," Malmgren explained. "And my left wrist is either broken or dislocated. How do you feel?"

"Apart from a slight discomfort in my left shoulder, I'm fine," Francis replied.

"We must find the general," Malmgren said.

Titina's barking led them directly to Nobile. The airship commander was sprawled out on the snow, his head covered in blood. First Officer Mariano was leaning over him, along with Alfredo, examining his injuries. Francis overheard the general say, "I think that I'm dying. Do all that you can to save the men."

But First Officer Mariano shook his head. "You've broken a leg and your wrist, General, and gashed your forehead. But you're still in command."

Francis gave an inward sigh of relief. If anyone could bring some measure of calm and order to such a nightmarish situation it was Nobile.

"All will be well," Francis said in a half whisper. "We'll be saved."

"I hope so," General Nobile replied with a weak smile, "for all your sakes."

Francis smiled in return, then gazed around him, trying to see how the other men were doing. First Officer Mariano was examining Cecioni, who was moaning in pain from a broken leg. Lying next to him was Zappi, the second-in-command and navigational officer. Zappi complained of a pain in his chest but was otherwise uninjured. Two other men were getting up—wireless operator Biagi and engineer Trojani. All seemed dazed, but not badly injured. Even Titina had emerged unharmed and in a playful mood. The little terrier was scampering across the ice pack, sniffing at pieces of wreckage and licking pieces of salty ice.

"That accounts for nine of us," Francis murmured. "But where's Pomella?"

Before he could ask Francis or Trojani to form a search party for the missing foreman motor mechanic, Biagi gave a shout. "The emergency radio's working! The field station's intact!"

Everyone immediately turned to him, those lying on the ice as well as those standing up. It filled them all with hope. Francis watched Biagi test the small set and then begin to search the immediate vicinity for other pieces of equipment to erect an aerial.

Alfredo stood beside Francis. "The key to our survival," he said, indicating the wireless transmitter. Both men realized that being able to communicate with their ship, the *Città di Milano*, stationed at King's Bay, would bring a rescue team within forty-eight hours. But even two days meant taking a grave risk with their lives. Out in the freezing cold without protection they wouldn't last long.

"Look!" First Officer Mariano shouted, holding something aloft. "I found a case of provisions."

"We won't starve," Francis said, then smiled bleakly. "But we might freeze to death."

Then, almost miraculously, General Nobile caught sight of something familiar half hidden between two ridges of ice. "An emergency sack! Mariano, get to it right away. You'll find valuable things inside, a silk tent and sleeping bag, some other survival gear and food."

Their chances of survival were increasing.

"Here! Over here!" Biagi suddenly shouted from behind a row of ice ridges. "I've found Pomella. He's dead. Killed by the impact."

Nobile closed his eyes, and silently said a prayer for his colleague.

"We need to cover his body in the snow," the general instructed, "until we can make him a more decent grave."

"I'll do it," Alfredo said.

"I'll help you," Francis offered.

While Mariano and Trojani set about erecting a double-walled tent on a level spot, Francis and Alfredo buried Pomella.

Francis's fingers were turning blue inside his gloves, while his feet felt like useless blocks of ice that burned with every move he made. When they had finished, the two men returned to the makeshift camp. Francis was pleased to see that Biagi had been able to construct an aerial from lengths of steel tubing that had broken loose from the *Italia*, and was ready to send out his call.

Nearly frozen, their faces drained of color, the

men gathered around the radio operator.

"SOS *Italia* . . . SOS *Italia* . . ." Biagi transmitted.

Francis, hearing these words, suddenly felt warmed despite the bitter temperatures and Arctic winds.

But there was no reply to the repeated SOS.

And then the set went dead.

"The Ice Is Splitting Beneath Us!"

The first night spent in the cold was agony.

We're lucky we have a tent, Alfredo thought, so we're not sleeping directly on the ice. The tent wasn't large, only eight feet by eight feet, held up by a pole in the center. It was designed for use by four men, and now nine crammed inside its confining space. Most of their equipment and food had to be stored inside the tent, also. But at least the walls and floor were lined with two layers of silk separated by a layer of air for added insulation. Even better, the floor was waterproof.

Alfredo jammed himself in next to Trojani and Biagi, huddling under the one thin blanket they possessed. The floor of the tent was as hard as cement, uneven and bumpy, and just as cold as the ice underneath it. All night long the polar wind howled across the ice, flapping the edge of the tent. The general woke often, moaning in pain from his injuries.

Cecioni couldn't get comfortable with his now splinted broken leg, and grumbled and cursed continuously. Titina would doze off next to her master, then waken with questioning barks at every creak of the tent or sound from the men. Just let us get through these nights, Alfredo prayed, so we can stay alive long enough to be rescued.

"Good news!" someone cried the next morning. "Biagi's got the radio working again."

They were sitting around a small fire, eating their breakfast rations of pemmican soup—a watery broth made from dried meat—and small bits of chocolate. Alfredo and Trojani cheered, while the other men put down their cups of broth to clap. The news couldn't have come at a better time, especially after the first grueling, sleepless night in the cold.

Biagi was stationed at his post a little distance from the tent, headphones on. He had erected a high mast for the aerial with all the steel tubing he could find in the snow. Attached to the top was a small strip of cloth, bearing the colors of Italy. He was about to begin transmitting again.

It wouldn't be long now, Alfredo thought, his spirits lifting. Someone will receive our distress calls and send out a rescue team.

Although Biagi didn't get a reply on this second day, the men performed their duties with renewed confidence and hope, and the first two days passed in a blur of activity and duties. First Officer Mariano became Nobile's second-in-command and ordered the men to stand watch, go out on additional search parties for equipment and provisions, and cook the meals.

Alfredo performed his assignments without question or complaint, but in a kind of disbelieving shock. *All* the men were in shock, Alfredo realized. The captain and crew of eight had literally been plucked out of the sky and tossed onto a stretch of uninhabited ice and snow with no experience in Arctic survival. Only Malmgren had any experience with these conditions. From 1922 to 1925 he had served on the Norwegian ice-ship *Maud* that had explored Alaska and the Siberian Islands. But his specialty was meteorology, not survival techniques.

Alfredo was dreaming of being in his mother's kitchen, relishing the smells and warmth coming from the cooking pots on the big stove, when he felt the earth move suddenly. Waking, he heard what sounded like a pistol shot, followed by a long vibrating roar. All the other men jerked awake.

"What . . . what is it?" Alfredo shouted.

"The pack is breaking up!" Malmgren said. "Everyone outside!"

"What did he say?" a terrified but still sleepy Trojani asked Alfredo.

"The ice is splitting beneath us," Alfredo hurriedly replied, jumping to his feet. "We've all got to move."

The thought of being swallowed alive by the ice made sweat break out on Alfredo's forehead despite the cold temperature. Panic flooded through all the men, but they still worked carefully together to half drag, half carry the injured Nobile and Cecioni outside. Alfredo held the flap open and then let it fall to join the others who had moved several yards from the tent. It was snowing lightly and he bounced up and down on the balls of his feet to keep warm. All they could do was wait. In another minute or two the floor of the ice could split right apart and toss them into the freezing black waters of the Arctic Ocean.

"How serious is the movement?" General Nobile asked. He was cradling his terrier in his arms as he lay on the ice.

"I don't know," Malmgren said soberly, "but if a break occurs near the tent, we should move immediately to another section of the pack, maybe a hundred yards to the east."

They waited in silence, shivering from the cold but also from panic. The terrible roaring sound of the ice cracking came closer and closer. It sounded like a locomotive relentlessly speeding in their direction. Alfredo could feel the soles of his booted feet trembling from the vibration. Fear raged in his stomach, although he tried to keep a calm and controlled expression on his face. It wouldn't do for a naval officer to crumble at the first sign of trouble. Unbelievably, the grinding noise of the ice stopped, leaving only a faraway echo. Alfredo exchanged wary looks with Malmgren and felt his heartbeat slow. The danger was over.

Silently the men returned to the tent and scrambled once again under the warmth of the one blanket. Two or three men talked nervously among themselves, while Alfredo tried to calm his breathing and fall back asleep.

It was a long while before he finally dozed off.

"There's a Bear!"

"You shouldn't be going!" Francis said forcefully. He stared at the faces of his companions around the fire and repeated, "You shouldn't be going. You can't leave the general and the rest of us without a senior officer."

"We've been arguing about this for two days now," First Officer Mariano retorted, "and more discussion isn't going to help. We *have* to organize a rescue party to march across the ice to get help."

"I know that the ice pack we're on has been shifting and moving—" Francis began.

"Twenty-eight miles to the southeast in just two days!" Malmgren interrupted him. "If we all stay here and do nothing, we're going to be floating out past Franz Joseph Land. Once we reach that, we'll never be found."

"But certainly someone's bound to pick up our SOS messages," Francis said.

"I can pick up transmissions from our ship," Biagi offered, "and even news bulletins from stations in Rome. But no one is monitoring *our* messages or signals."

"You heard what the President of the Italian Senate said last night in his broadcast," First Officer Mariano heatedly said. "He expressed deep sorrow for the crew of the *Italia*, which had 'sacrificed itself' for science. Don't you see what that means, Francis? Our country thinks we're dead. They're not going to look for us."

"We've got to do *something*," Mariano urged. "We can't just sit here, waiting to die."

Finally it was decided. The two most senior officers, Mariano and Zappi, were to leave the next morning, along with Malmgren.

Francis crept into the tent that night, tired out from the never-ending discussion and argument. When would the turmoil cease? he wondered bitterly. Five days of confinement on the ice pack and tempers were beginning to flare. He tossed and turned that night, worrying about Malmgren's going on the trek the next day. The meteorologist was the only one among the men whose knowledge of the Arctic could help them survive. Hoping against hope that his friend would experience a change of heart and back out of the patrol, Francis finally dozed off.

Suddenly, he was awakened by someone crawling into the tent. "There's a bear!" the man whispered.

Instantly, all the men woke up.

"Where—where is it?" Francis blurted.

He jerked his head jerked around, as if expecting (and dreading) to find the bear in the tent.

Zappi gave a tense laugh. "Not here, outside the tent."

"A bear . . ." The men began murmuring in soft voices. One by one they got up and slipped into their coats and boots. A wave of tension, of anticipation, crackled through the air.

"We could use the meat," Mariano declared with a gleam in his eye.

"You're not thinking of going out there and trying to hunt that—*thing*!" Francis said in shock. He turned to look at Zappi. "How big is it?"

Zappi raised a hand high above his head.

Francis sank back against the mattress. No one was going to be foolhardy enough to risk going up against a beast of that size, he thought. Look at it, maybe. From some safe distance away. But hunt it . . . ? Well, don't ask me, he thought, nervously licking his lips. I'm sure no one else is crazy enough to go out there either.

But Malmgren jumped up and got the pistol from General Nobile.

"I'm going to hunt it," he calmly announced.

"No!" Francis declared, shaking his head. "It's too dangerous! Don't do it!"

But his friend merely glanced at him with a daring smile as he loaded the pistol. As soon as that was done, Malmgren crept outside. Francis watched as the others silently and cautiously followed. Legs trembling, hands clenched into fists, he took a shaky breath and stepped outside. Even the injured Cecioni and the general dragged themselves out of the tent, helped by Zappi and Trojani. Nobile had picked up Titina and cradled her head against his chest to stop her from barking and alarming the bear.

The sun was beginning to shine on this bitterly cold predawn morning. There was enough light to easily spot the bear, standing partially hidden behind some ice ridges about thirty yards from the tent. The animal, a huge polar bear standing more than eight feet tall, stared back at the ragtag assortment of humans. Its tiny black eyes glittered from the reflection of the ice. They could see its thick black claws—bladed weapons able to shred human skin.

Francis huddled inside his coat. One sudden move and the bear would attack. Despite the weapons the men had brought with them—an ax, a knife, steel tubing, a nail, a file—they were all frightened. Not one of them had ever been this close to a bear before, except in a zoo.

Malmgren motioned for them to stay behind until he got close enough to take aim at the bear. Mariano and Zappi crept a little closer, armed with an ax and a knife in case the gun jammed or Malmgren missed. Both men's faces were tense, their eyes never leaving the bear.

Closer and closer Malmgren approached until he was only ten yards away. The polar bear didn't move. He simply stood there, wagging his head back and forth. Malmgren took aim and fired—once, twice, three times just to be sure. The animal turned and lumbered a few paces, then collapsed on the ice.

"Got him!" the general cried.

Alfredo held up a hand, motioning for them to wait. He went to examine the fallen bear. He leaned over, then raised a fist.

"Dead," he announced and his face broke into a grin.

A collective sigh of relief went up from the men. Several nervously laughed.

"Let's skin it and cut it up while it's still warm," Malmgren advised. "There should be over four hundred pounds of meat for us to eat, and the skin will come in handy for a rug or blanket."

The men got to work while Francis helped carry the general back inside the tent.

"Don't you see what a blessing this is?" Nobile said to Francis. "With all the food we have now, Mariano and the others won't have to leave right away. They can stay and monitor the wireless transmissions."

But a few hours later First Officer Mariano came into the tent with Zappi and Malmgren beside him. They told the general of their resolve to leave the camp that very evening.

"They've Heard Us!"

Alfredo was assigned new responsibilities by General Nobile. The first was making solar observations when the weather was clear enough to take sights. The second was the preservation and distribution of food. The bear that Malmgren had shot was cut into large chunks and hung up in waterproof canvas from the wreck of the airship cabin. Alfredo then tied the bear meat packets at intervals along a rope, just in case the ice pack broke apart, and food got tossed into the ocean. This way any packet that fell into the water would be saved because it was attached to others still on the ice.

Many times Alfredo secretly wished the packets of bear meat would tumble into the Arctic Ocean and float away. He was sick of bear. It was served boiled at lunch, and roasted for dinner. It didn't matter how it was prepared, it was awful. Leathery, tasteless, and greasy. Only Titina, Nobile's pet terrier, seemed to gobble down her portions with any enjoyment.

The survivors went about life on the ice pack quietly. Even usually good-natured Francis had stopped struggling to communicate in Italian, and took to fishing on the canal in silence. Alfredo tried to remain positive at all times, as much to keep Nobile's spirits up as well as his own. There were times when he glimpsed the anxiety, almost panic, behind Nobile's orders.

On June 3, four days after the search party had left, Alfredo noticed a marked change in the drift of the ice pack. He reported it to General Nobile.

"The current is sweeping us closer to land than we had hoped for!" he exclaimed. "My calculations show we're only four miles north-northeast of Foyn Island and five miles northeast of Broch."

Foyn and Broch were two islands in the Arctic region that tortured the men with their closeness one week, their distance the next. If their ice pack continued to swing in either island's direction, however, the men would need to undertake just a short march to solid land.

"Keep an eye on our drift and report to me tomorrow," the general advised.

Unfortunately, the current proved to be an enemy. When Alfredo took his observation the next morning, he was crushed to discover that they were *farther* away from the islands than ever. Would they *never* escape from this nightmare? Alfredo thought in despair. Just when salvation looked within reach, it cruelly floated away. He trudged back to the general to report this crushing news.

"We must continue to rely on the radio," Nobile told Alfredo. "We can never hope to make it across the ice now."

To Alfredo, however, as well as to the other men, the radio had lost its once-magical promise of rescue. Biagi had been transmitting nonstop for ten days, and there was not the slightest indication that the SOS signals had been heard. They had also begun to question the effectiveness of the three-man patrol.

"If they marched as far each day as Malmgren thought they would, they would have easily reached land by now," Cecioni complained. "But we still hear nothing."

No one wanted to voice the fear that the three men had lost their lives, and all for nothing.

On June 5, Alfredo decided to ask the general's permission to organize their own march. The weather had turned ugly and the southward drift continued at an alarming rate.

"Very soon," Alfredo confided, "we'll be *beyond* Foyn and Broch Islands, and past Cape Leigh Smith. Once that happens, General, we'll be in uncharted waters, where there's no chance of reaching land."

He was just about to ask the general to let them attempt the march to land, when he realized it wouldn't do any good. General Nobile's lips were drawn together in a bitter, resigned line. Their leader and commander thought the end was near.

The six survivors went to sleep that night feeling helpless. Alfredo lay awake in the tent, watching Nobile glance at his pistol from time to time. Had it come to this? Was it better to take their own lives than to prolong a painful and drawn-out end?

The next evening Biagi was at his radio, ready to send out his standard message at 8 P.M. The rest of the men dejectedly picked at their roasted bear meat, hardly saying a word. The wireless operator put his headphones on and said, "Well, here we go again," without any hope.

"SOS *Italia*, Nobile," he painstakingly tapped out. "On the ice near Foyn Island, northeast Spitzbergen. Impossible to move, lacking sleds and having two men injured. Dirigible lost in another locality. Reply via Ido 32." Ido 32 was a code word Biagi used for San Paolo, the Italian station that came in so clearly.

He sent the message for almost an hour, then turned his receiver in on the San Paolo news broadcasts. He waited, his notebook and pencil motionless in his hands.

"They've heard us!" Biagi suddenly shouted.

Everyone froze. They waited as Biagi began scribbling furiously, listening to the message. Alfredo jumped to his feet and and stared over the shoulder of the wireless operator as the words formed.

The Soviet Embassy . . . has informed the Italian government that . . . an SOS from the Italia *. . . has been picked up by a young Soviet farmer . . . Nicholas Schmidt, at Archangel . . . on the evening of June third . . .*

Alfredo burst out laughing. It seemed impossible, too good to be true, but it had happened. Someone with a ham radio had heard the faint and mangled message more than 1,200 miles away from the ice pack.

"We're going to be saved," Alfredo said. "Saved!"

He picked up Trojani and swung him around and around.

The "Red Tent"

Francis paced in the snow, his eyes scanning the horizon.

He was on guard duty tonight, two days after the wonderful news that their SOS had been heard. The entire camp's morale had improved dramatically, and even having to stand out in the bitter cold when everyone else was snugly inside the tent didn't bother the scientist at all. It was exciting to gaze out at the horizon, because help could be on its way. It could appear in the air or on the sea. What an honor it would be to be the first to sight the rescue team, Francis thought.

Francis slapped his arms against his lambskin coat to keep warm. It wasn't so bad as long as he kept moving, but his feet were aching from the cold. The Eskimo boots they all wore were not meant for extended periods on the snow and ice. Only Biagi had been smart enough—or just lucky enough—to have slipped on leather-soled shoes during the flight, and that kept his feet protected and warm.

At least his stomach was full, Francis thought with a grin. After the men celebrated two nights ago around the fire, the general had ordered their extra rations of chocolate and sugar be handed out.

General Nobile had also ordered them to paint the tent with wide red stripes, using dye from several unbroken altitude "bombs." These were glass balls filled with red liquid that were sent hurtling from the airship onto the snow below in order to determine the aircraft's altitude. Now their little shelter, once so muddy and drab, became a beacon of hope to the men. The "red tent" would surely attract the attention of any planes flying overhead.

Wait, what was that?

Francis stopped humming. Was that a crack in the ice? Or could it be a large polar bear, prowling around camp? He strained to listen, then grunted when he realized the noise was coming from the tent.

"What's happening?" Francis demanded, poking his head inside the flap.

"They're calling us! They're calling us!" Biagi shouted.

"Who's calling?" Francis said.

"Rome!" Biagi cried.

"No, it can't be." General Nobile shook his head and frowned. "You must have heard wrong."

"Yes, it's Rome."

As Biagi began to translate the sound into letters and words, the Italian members of the crew waited. Francis noted the softening of the expressions on the faces of the grimy, bearded men. This was their homeland making contact from 3,000 miles away. Now their families would learn they were alive.

The next morning Biagi made contact again.

"Be ready to make a smoke signal," the message from Rome instructed them. "Airplanes will be—"

"Will be *what*?" Francis asked impatiently.

"It's too jumbled to decipher," Biagi replied. "I can't make it out."

General Nobile instructed Biagi to respond: "We will make smoke signals and fire Very lights as the airplanes approach. Remember that our batteries may run out in a few days, but we will still be able to receive." He also had Biagi mention their position on the ice pack, information on the weather, and the fact that three of their companions were marching east along the coast toward Cape North.

"Our rescue is only a few days away!" Francis predicted.

"A plane or a ship is sure to be on its way to us right now," Biagi added.

Cecioni burst into snatches of opera, much to everyone's groans or laughter, and the men fantasized aloud about the first thing they would do once they were home.

But just at the peak of their joy, near-disaster struck.

On June 9, General Nobile instructed Alfredo to break out the Very lights and pistol. Since Francis had never witnessed this display before, he joined the others in the tent to see how the Very pistol was loaded. Alfredo quickly located and examined the cartridges that would shoot the colored balls of fire into the sky, but returned them to the general with a glum expression.

"They don't fit," he explained. "These cartridges are for another pistol, which we don't have."

Francis watched Nobile examine them himself, then curse softly.

"How can we signal airplanes of our location without a flare?" the general said. He thought a moment. "Just to be on the safe side, we should begin to collect oily rags, bear grease, and extra gasoline to light a smudge fire if an airplane approaches."

Cecioni held out his hand. "Let me try to file the cartridges down to fit inside the pistol," he offered. He began smoothing the edges of the cartridges with a rusty file from his kit. Francis and the others watched his painstaking process.

Suddenly, the head of the cartridge flew off, bounced on the floor of the tent, and exploded in a flash of smoke and flame. A piece of the silk lining caught fire. Francis watched a portion of the tent erupt in a blaze. A gasp squeezed out of his throat, yet he found himself too shocked to move, to act.

General Nobile ripped off his jacket and smothered the blaze before it could spread. The tent was unharmed. Cecioni had lightly scorched the palm of his hand, but he was not seriously injured.

Francis left the tent and walked in circles. At first he felt numb after the near tragedy, but then anger began churning in his stomach. Churning and boiling, about to erupt.

"How long can we go on like this?" Francis screamed in rage to the sky above. "How long?"

They had blown the one good opportunity they had to alert a rescue expedition of their location. Would they ever get a second chance, or were they to be stranded forever on the ice?

"The Ice Is Splitting Right Toward Us!"

"We may have to move soon, General," Alfredo said. "The ice on all sides of us has large cracks that are growing wider each hour."

Alfredo had returned from his daily midmorning inspection.

"How bad is it?" Nobile asked. He was lying inside the tent, cradling a sleeping Titina.

"The weather's changed in the last three days," Alfredo reported. "Strong west winds are driving the ice eastward at the rate of five to six miles a day. You can hear the sound of ice fracturing constantly. I'm afraid if we don't move the tent, the ice is going to split directly under us."

Nobile bit his lip in frustration. "I hate to have the men pack up all the equipment and shift camp, but there really isn't a choice, is there?"

Alfredo frowned and shook his head. "No, General."

Nobile was upset over the news, so Alfredo decided not to tell him that a dense fog was sweeping over the open waters to the west. It had been so thick this morning that Alfredo had found it impossible to see more than one hundred yards in front of him. For a few moments, he had lost his way back to the tent. If the fog continued to spread, rescue teams wouldn't be able to spot them from a distance.

Alfredo kept the news to himself and joined the others in packing the equipment. Everyone had been cheered up by the promise of a rescue four days ago, but since then nothing had happened. Biagi had continued to send out daily coordinates as their position moved southward, and he received messages that always said the same thing: Help is on the way.

But which way? What kind of help were they talking about? Although they constantly scanned the horizon, no ships were ever spotted. Alfredo told the men to look for smoke first, and then the vessel would follow. General Nobile had grown increasingly worried over the delay. Provisions were dwindling. He had Biagi wire for rations of pemmican, rifles, and, most essential, a collapsible boat. With the rate the ice was melting all around them, the survivors might soon end up in the ocean.

Francis was helping Alfredo take down the lines of bear meat when he suddenly paused and held up his hand.

"Listen," he said. "I think I hear a plane!"

Everyone froze. Alfredo made out a humming noise. It could have been the sound of a distant engine. But Biagi groaned and pointed to the radio antenna. The little Italian flag attached to the top was vibrating in the heavy wind.

"No plane," the wireless operator said in a flat voice.

The men got back to work.

Someone screamed, "The ice! The ice is splitting right toward us!"

Piercing booms exploded, followed by a dramatic shuddering of the ice.

"What's happening out there?" Cecioni cried.

Alfredo rushed into the tent. "A channel is forming. We'll have to move right away."

He moved quickly, carrying both Cecioni and the general out of the tent. The force of the wind and the current had opened a canal ten yards wide that seemed to be heading directly to the tent. Any second and the next heave of the ice could swallow up the tent, supplies, and men if they didn't move fast enough.

But once again luck was against them. A dense

icy white mist swirled around the ice. Everywhere the men turned, gaps opened at their feet. Supplies toppled into the cracks, and they had to fish them out.

"Hurry! *Hurry!*" they screamed at each other. Gasping for breath, the men worked in a rapid frenzy of activity. The two injured men had to be lifted onto a crude stretcher and lugged across ice ridges and dirty, watery puddles.

"Grab the dog!" General Nobile shouted as Titina scampered across the ice. Alfredo spun around and took off after her, slipping and falling painfully to his knees in his haste.

"Come here, Titina!" Alfredo commanded. The terrier was so frightened by the noise that she ran straight into his arms.

By the time camp had been set up one hundred feet away on a more solid stretch of ice, Alfredo was exhausted. He and the men collapsed inside the tent.

"Now," the general ordered, "set up the radio."

Biagi put on his headphones and bent over the radio. Almost immediately, the expression on his face told the men something was wrong.

"What?" Cecioni demanded. "Biagi, what is it?"

The wireless operator hesitated. He looked around the tent at each of the men.

"We've been cut off," he said in a quiet voice. "Our batteries are finally giving out."

Sighted at Last!

Four days crept by without any sign of a ship or a plane. The winds died down and the weather improved. The sun shone every day under cloudless blue skies. The men took turns scanning the horizon, sometimes staring into the sun for hours at a time. No one talked about rescue. They were silent, sunk in their own thoughts. Biagi had been able to push some messages through despite the weakening batteries, although the *Città* had failed to respond.

On June 17, Francis was outside with Biagi when he caught sight of a bear. It was another polar bear, but this bear was not standing still. It was pawing over the grave of Pomella. It unearthed an arm.

The two men looked at each other, terrified to move, to breathe, to call attention to themselves.

"Get the pistol," Biagi whispered.

Francis nodded and hurried inside the tent.

Hoping he looked braver than he felt, he blurted, "There's a bear outside. We need the pistol."

Trojani, the frail little bespectacled engineer, jumped to his feet. "Let me do it," he implored.

Grateful for the offer, Francis followed Trojani outside and crept along slowly beside him. Heart thudding, Francis hoped that Trojani was as good a shot as Malmgren. They edged up ten yards, twenty yards, until Trojani was in range.

Luckily the bear was so engrossed in his own activity that he failed to catch the scent of the men. But any moment now that could change, Francis realized.

He watched Trojani raise the gun, take aim, and fire.

He missed.

The bear swung around and growled. He glared at the two men.

"Take another shot," Francis hissed.

Trojani's hands were shaking, but he managed to aim and fire. The bullet grazed the animal's shoulder. Now the bear rose on its hind legs and bared its teeth.

It's going to attack, Francis realized. Turning and running would only goad the bear into chasing them. Trojani fumbled with the pistol.

A tiny dark shape streaked into view and halted a

few feet in front of the polar bear. Titina was defending her master and her territory. Barking and growling, the terrier rose to her hind legs and confronted the huge animal. At any other time the sight would have reduced him to tears of helpless laughter, but Francis didn't find it funny or ridiculous now because the polar bear had fallen back on all fours and was pacing back and forth as if he was about to pounce.

Titina snarled, then jumped forward.

The bear bellowed, then turned on its heels and fled.

Francis sagged in relief. Titina trotted back over to him. He grabbed her up and kissed her wet nose. "You saved our lives," he declared. "Tonight you get my malted-milk ration."

"She's a hero," Trojani agreed. "Wait until we tell the general."

As they headed back to the tent, a strange sound made Francis look up.

"Planes, planes!" he shouted. He pointed at the sky. "Two planes, coming from the south!"

The men farther out on the ice pack heard his cries and began running back to camp.

Nobile dragged himself to the entrance of the tent. "Break out the Very pistol and light a fire. Trojani, start your smudge fire."

The two planes circled overhead in a search pattern, but didn't zero in on the men.

"They should have seen the signal," Officer Viglieri said with a frown. "I fired two lights in the air."

"Perhaps it's too bright out," Nobile offered, trying to mask his disappointment. "The sun, the bright sky, even the reflection from the ice could absorb the Very light."

Trojani fanned the flames of the smudge fire, but only produced a thin wisp of sooty smoke that quickly disappeared in the wind.

"The planes are going away," Francis said in numb disbelief. "They're flying away."

He stumbled a few paces in the snow, looking up into the sky. "Come back," he muttered. "Come back! Don't leave us here!"

On June 18 the men were informed on the radio that another rescue attempt would be made. Norwegian tri-motor planes would be taking off as soon as the engines were changed. Early that afternoon Alfredo scouted for a possible landing field smooth enough for a light plane, and reported back that he had found the perfect site not far from camp. He and Biagi marked the stretch of flat ice with four flags. Then they waited.

On June 19 the men spotted two planes cruising

high overhead, but they never came closer than about four miles. Frustration warred constantly with hope among the men. One hour they were certain that today would be their last day on the ice pack. The next hour they'd be staring savagely into the smudge fire, Very pistol in hand, waiting in vain for any sight or sound of aircraft.

On June 20, twenty-seven days after being stranded on the ice, Francis spotted an S-55 hydroplane piloted by Italian officers at seven-thirty in the morning.

"There she is!" Francis shouted.

"Light the fire," Nobile ordered.

Relying on radio instructions from a wireless on board the plane, the pilots were able this time to zero in on the small band of men. The plane circled, then dipped directly over them. Francis could actually make out the head of the pilot in the cockpit. The pilot was able to see him, too. He smiled at Francis and waved. Other members of the plane's crew peered out the cabin windows to wave at the survivors. Everyone on the ice pack burst out into a joyous celebration. Even Titina sensed the excitement, barking wildly, and dashing back and forth over the floes.

"We're saved!" Trojani cried, falling to his knees.

"Look, they're tossing out provisions," Nobile

said. "Go and get them before they fall into the cracks."

This is it, Francis thought. This is the day we're lifted off the ice. The big airplane droned overhead after making several passes, and then soared into the distance, its engine roar decreasing. The men lifted their beaming, grinning faces to watch the plane's wings bank into a turn for a return run. But the plane never banked it wings or made the turn. It went straight on, then wheeled in the wrong direction.

"What's happened?" Biagi demanded. "Why isn't it returning?"

Trojani let out a lone anguished wail and collapsed on the ice.

"It's not coming back," he said in a barely audible voice. He cast a hopeless glance at the men. "Don't you understand? There's no place to touch down safely. That's why they turned around and left."

Only Room for One

Three days passed.

The men were located again by other planes, although they, too, never landed. They simply dropped off provisions, then flew away. The men received packages containing bananas and lemons, boxes of cigarettes, medical supplies, rifles and ammunition, batteries, and, much to Alfredo's great pleasure, a pair of extra-large leather shoes that fit him perfectly. Alfredo thought it was ironic that he'd get warm shoes just when he'd be getting off the ice pack, but he didn't care. He might as well enjoy a small luxury like this in the short time remaining than go without and suffer from the cold.

"Soon now," the men kept telling themselves. Alfredo found a note pinned to the brown paper wrapping of one packet: *From the Swedish Expedition, Ostra Gruppen: If you can find a landing field for planes fitted with skis (minimum 250 yards), arrange the red parachutes in a T-shape on the leeward side.*

This confirmed their thoughts on why the airplanes circled overhead, but never landed. The condition of the ice was so bad it would be impossible for any aircraft to safely touch down, except for an extremely light ski-plane.

Spirits remained high, but problems were developing. The weather had warmed so much that the ice was melting and cracking at an increasing rate. If they weren't lifted off soon, the men wouldn't have a strong solid base to hold them.

Alfredo and the general discussed their chances of survival if the planes failed to return soon.

"We'll have to take the collapsible boats out," Nobile said, "and load them with supplies and provisions."

But Alfredo wasn't so sure. "We'd be lucky to get them into the water without capsizing," he faltered. "Once we were in the boats we'd still be faced with the task of fighting the wind and currents to reach land."

The general gave a resigned shrug. "We don't have a choice if the ice starts to go."

And it could go soon, Alfredo thought uneasily. They didn't have more than a day or two at most. Hiding his worry as best he could, he joined the others around the fire for a late dinner.

Alfredo bit into a chunk of leathery bear meat, pretending it was steak, when he heard something that made him stop chewing. The others caught it, too—a distant humming sound that seemed to be increasing.

Planes!

The general snapped out an order: "Light a smoke signal. And Officers Viglieri and Biagi, go to the landing site and help direct the pilot."

Alfredo and Biagi were on their feet in a flash, their rations tumbling to the ground. The two men stumbled, hopped, and slipped their way across the ice to get to the markers.

"What do you think?" Biagi shouted, glancing across his post at Alfredo. "Do you think this time we'll be lucky?"

Alfredo squinted upward. Two planes droned overhead, a big hydroplane accompanied by a smaller Fokker military biplane equipped with runners. If all went well, the little biplane would be able to touch down successfully.

"Say a prayer!" Alfredo said.

Both men, as well as those stationed by the tent, kept their eyes glued to the Fokker. It circled the encampment several times, touching down low to assess the landing conditions. Then it glided in again, losing height slowly until it seemed to skim the snow.

The runners touched down and then clattered across the rough ice until the plane glided to a safe stop. It was June 23, at exactly eleven o'clock at night.

Biagi and Alfredo sprinted across the snowy landing field to the plane. When the pilot climbed down, a big, rugged-looking Swedish man in his early thirties, the two men warmly clutched at him. Another man remained in the cockpit, the engine ticking over. The second plane, the massive hydroplane, circled lazily overhead, unable to find a safe stretch of water on which to land.

The pilot glanced across at the tent and at General Nobile, awkwardly balancing against the entrance.

"Can the general walk?" the pilot asked.

Both Alfredo and Biagi shook their heads, still so out of breath that they couldn't talk.

"Then we shall have to go and help him."

The three men picked their way across the lumpy, uneven terrain until they reached the tent.

"Here is the general!" Alfredo announced proudly.

Nobile embraced the pilot with tears in his eyes.

"I am Lieutenant Lundborg of the Swedish Air Force," the pilot said in English, saluting. "I have come to fetch you. The field is good, and I'll be able to take away *all* of you during the night, but you must come first."

Nobile firmly shook his head. "That's impossible. I've already instructed that my mechanic, Natale Cecioni, be evacuated first. He's badly injured."

"No," the pilot protested, equally as forcefully. "I have orders to take you first, because we need you to advise us how to search for the other men who are missing. Our base isn't far from here. I can come back quickly for the others."

But General Nobile continued to argue with Lundborg. Alfredo thought he knew the real reason behind the general's insistence on staying behind. It wouldn't befit an officer of such high rank if he chose to be evacuated first. It might appear that he was deserting his men, and Alfredo realized that General Nobile would never willingly leave the men who had come to depend upon him as a father figure, as well as a commander.

But the Swedish pilot was vehement in his orders.

"You come with me now, we have no time to lose. Come, General," he impatiently barked, "this is not grand opera."

Finally, after much discussion with the men, who insisted that Nobile go, the general reluctantly gave in. Clutching Titina in his arms, Nobile said an emotional farewell to his men.

Alfredo shook the general's hand, sad that their leader and pillar of support would be leaving them, but eager for the pilot to return to evacuate them all off the ice.

"Good-bye," said Nobile with tears in his eyes. "I will see you in a little while."

But it would be a long time before the survivors saw the general again.

For them, the nightmare was only beginning.

"He's Going to Hit the Ice!"

Francis jotted scientific observations in his log book, then glanced across at Trojani. The engineer moaned on the floor of the tent, consumed by fever and bad stomach cramps.

"Are you all right?" Francis said. "Can I get you any water?"

Trojani shook his head. He gazed at Francis with worried, burning eyes. "What's taking so long? Why hasn't the pilot returned?"

"He'll be back," Francis said confidently. "We'll hear the plane any minute now. It hasn't been long."

Trojani nodded weakly, then closed his eyes. After a while his breathing became more measured and he fell asleep.

Francis tossed his log book on the ground and stood up. He had been sitting here for hours—too many hours to keep pretending any longer that everything was all right. He had told Trojani that he

needn't worry, but he lied. The Swedish pilot Lundborg had said that base camp was close by, an hour or so away. So why was it taking so long for him to return?

Finally, Francis heard the sound of someone returning to camp. At last, he thought in relief. Word that the plane's been sighted. But it was only a scowl-faced Biagi who stormed over to his radio.

"What's happening?" Francis said.

Biagi threw up his hands in frustration. "It's been three hours since the plane left with the general. Something's wrong. I'm going to try to radio our ship to have them relay a message to the Swedish Air Force to find out what's delaying Lundborg."

But luck, once again, was not on the survivors' side. Biagi was unable to get through to the ship. After thirty minutes of useless transmitting, he yanked off his headphones and grimaced at Francis.

"No use," he declared. "I'm heading back to the landing site."

"I'll stay here with Trojani," Francis said.

He watched Biagi slip and slide his way across the bumpy ice. Frustrated beyond belief, Francis pulled his gloves off and hurled them across the snow. Get me off this awful island, he thought bitterly, and I swear I'll never go up in an airship again.

Alfredo was now first in command.

As soon as Nobile had flown off in the biplane, Alfredo instructed Cecioni to come to the landing strip in order to be ready when the pilot returned. With Biagi's assistance, Alfredo helped Cecioni drag himself across the ice on his new crutches. At one point Cecioni slipped and had to be pulled out of the icy water. He was soaked and considerably miserable by the time he finally arrived at the site.

Three hours later he was even more miserable when Biagi returned from the tent.

"I'm sorry, but there's no word about the Swedish pilot," Biagi stated. "I can't get through to the ship."

Alfredo bit back an explosive retort. He had to display the same kind of quiet, positive outlook that General Nobile would have encouraged.

"It's all right," he reassured the two men. "We'll be rescued by the end of the day."

But Biagi didn't seem to share his confidence. He paced nervously over the flat icy stretch, eyes fixed constantly on the horizon.

"What could be wrong?" he asked repeatedly. "It's clear weather. The Swedes have our exact coordinates. And the general certainly wouldn't allow the rescue to delay returning to us."

Three more grueling hours passed. Cecioni lay back on the ice under the bear skin for insulation, mumbling under his breath. Biagi continued to mutter and pace. Alfredo paced, too, but suddenly paused.

"Listen," he said. "I think I hear it—the plane."

All eyes immediately scanned the horizon. Yes, there was the Fokker biplane, circling high in the air. He had started his glide in low over the ice, but he wasn't judging the distance properly.

"What's wrong with him?" Biagi burst out.

The plane kept coming, cutting its landing distance dangerously in half. It wouldn't have enough room to touch down properly.

"Get down, get down!" Alfredo screamed. "Can't that idiotic fool see he's overshooting the mark?"

Biagi waved his arms wildly. "Go on up and try it all over again!"

Cecioni thrust a crutch into the air. "Go up! Go up!" he yelled.

But it was too late. The ski-like runners had touched down. The plane bumped crazily along the ice at high speed.

"He's going to hit the ice!" Cecioni shouted in alarm.

The small biplane caught on a block of ice just beyond the designated runway and crashed upside down, its propeller smashed.

Alfredo and Biagi rushed over to the plane. The engine was still, but a little puddle of oil leaked from it steadily onto the ice. Lundborg cursed loudly in his native language and wriggled free from the cockpit to lower himself to safety.

"Are you all right?" Alfredo said.

Lundborg didn't respond. He turned and began kicking and pounding the body of the plane.

Suddenly it became clear—Lundborg was drunk.

"You pig!" Cecioni shouted at the pilot. "You couldn't wait until rescuing the rest of us before celebrating!"

Alfredo put a restraining hand on his friend's shoulder. Struggling to disguise his own outrage, he walked over to Lundborg. By now the pilot's drunken fury had died down and he wore an embarrassed, gloomy expression.

"You better go to the tent and lie down for a while," Alfredo suggested.

Lundborg nodded, then quietly followed Biagi back to the encampment.

"What about me?" Cecioni demanded. "I'm frozen from sitting on the wet ice."

"Don't worry, I'll get you back to camp so you can dry off," Alfredo said, but his eyes were fixed on the tipped-over biplane.

This was their one chance to end the nightmare and get back to civilization. Now their way out was smashed to pieces, just like their hopes of survival. If the weather got worse, rescue planes couldn't land on the ice, and if the ice continued to melt, it would only be a matter of time before they'd all go under. Alfredo's skin crawled with cold, the kind of cold that had nothing to do with the temperature.

One New Survivor
Spells Trouble

At six o'clock in the morning on June 29, Alfredo stepped back to check the latest set of solar observations when he felt his feet sink into the ice. Startled, he looked down and realized that many areas of the landing strip were becoming covered with water. If any plane did manage to arrive, it would be extremely dangerous to touch down, and almost impossible to take off again. His worst fears were being realized.

"Please let a plane land soon," Alfredo fervently prayed. "It has to be *soon*."

For the last five days the men were constantly seesawing between having their hopes raised to seeing them shattered. Each morning Biagi would look up cheerfully from the radio to announce good news: planes were departing from King's Bay, or from the Swedish base at Virgo Bay, or from the camp of the Norwegians. But inevitably heavy fog would start rolling in until visibility was reduced to less than half a mile, and all rescue operations were called off. But at least the men were used to the up-and-down conditions by now, Alfredo thought. It was their newest addition who couldn't take the stress.

He shook his head as he began to make his way back to camp. Ever since Einar Lundborg had literally dropped into their midst, he had spelled nothing but trouble. The Swedish pilot had questioned his orders right from the start and then collapsed into an infectious depression that soon spread to the others.

Lundborg had affected the state of mind of each man—and not for the better. Trojani had become sad and withdrawn, Cecioni outspoken and surly, Francis quiet and obsessed with his journals. Only Biagi and Alfredo had maintained a hopeful outlook. Biagi was a natural-born optimist anyway, while Alfredo, as the leader, couldn't let down his morale.

But what was he going to do about the more pressing problem of the condition of the ice? By his calculations, the men were nine miles off land, the last land they'd sight if the ice continued to move to the southeast.

Alfredo came into camp and instructed Biagi to radio their position. Perhaps the cloaked plea for help would motivate the Swedes or Norwegians to risk a rescue operation. But once again word came back that visibility was poor and they'd have to wait.

"But we can't wait any longer!" Lundborg forcefully interjected. "The only hope left for us is to make a march across the ice."

Alfredo listened to Lundborg's arguments for an entire day. That evening he allowed the pilot to transmit to Nobile his request to make a march to the *Città*. The men waited impatiently for the general's response. It came immediately.

"Four planes are ready to start and only wait until visibility is a little better. My opinion is that you should wait there and try not to walk. Please say whether you think that conditions of the field are good enough for landing tomorrow."

Lundborg jumped up with a surly frown and stalked out of the tent. The men exchanged unhappy glances with each other, shaking their heads.

Alfredo later received a private communication from the general. "Do not, under any circumstances," it read, "allow the men to leave the camp. Planes are ready at several bases to fly as soon as visibility permits. And the *Krassin* is on her way." (The *Krassin* was a Russian ship, the most powerful icebreaker in Europe.)

Another would-be disaster averted, Alfredo thought. Lundborg had accepted the general's opinion (for now) and didn't press for leaving. But how long would he continue to wait if the expected planes or ship failed to appear? How long could they all wait?

But the planes never appeared.

The *Krassin* failed to arrive.

Waiting became an agony. Nerves were rubbed raw. To add to the men's misery, a raging storm hit the ice pack. For five days cyclonic winds battered the Arctic Ocean, while sleet, hail, and snow pelted the survivors without mercy. Underneath them, the ice groaned and shuddered.

The survivors huddled, shivering, inside their dirty, frayed coats, never feeling warm, never feeling dry.

"I don't think I can take it anymore," Lundborg declared in a tight, yet almost trembling voice one night. They were sitting around a fire that constantly threatened to go out. "I'm going to kill myself if I have to stay here another day."

Francis turned a startled face to the pilot. Lundborg was serious. Lundborg was rapidly losing his will to live as the days passed and no planes appeared.

"Have patience," Francis said softly. "We all must have patience."

But Lundborg only grunted and turned his face away.

On July 5, the storm vanished and the sunshine returned. Biagi radioed General Nobile on board the *Città* that conditions were excellent for a landing. Later that day Francis saw seaplanes overhead. They dropped more provisions but also seemed to be checking on the condition of the landing strip.

"What are they doing? Why aren't they coming in?" Lundborg exclaimed in panic.

"Just hold on a little longer," Francis assured him.

At 2 A.M. the following morning, Francis was awakened by an excited Alfredo.

"A small plane has landed!" he shouted into the tent, waking up Lundborg and the others. "Is it one of your pilots?"

Lundborg raced outside the tent. "Yes!" he exclaimed. "It's a small British Moth!"

"How many people will it hold?" Biagi asked.

"Only two," Lundborg replied, "the pilot and one passenger."

Francis and the other survivors exchanged disheartened glances. It was all too obvious who should be evacuated next—not Cecioni, who had been waiting so patiently, but the overwrought, suicidal Lundborg. Alfredo instructed the now weeping Swedish pilot to get his belongings together and board the tiny plane. Francis followed Alfredo over to the pilot who was checking the outside of the plane for any signs of damage.

"When will you or the other pilots be coming back to get us?" Alfredo said.

But the pilot couldn't give him any definite answers. He avoided their eyes as he talked, and spoke in an unsteady voice. Suddenly it became clear to Francis what was wrong.

The strain of Arctic flying, the uncertainties of the weather, the dangers of landing on hazardous sites were beginning to take a terrible toll on the pilots. Judging by this man's pale, frightened face and shaky hands, he wouldn't be returning, Francis realized. Certainly Lundborg would never come back. And the rest of the pilots would be just as unwilling to risk their necks for a ragtag band of Italian survivors—*if their own countrymen weren't making the effort to save them.*

Francis knew that what meant. They were doomed to remain on the ice pack for an indefinite length of time. Judging by the near-broken spirits of the men, Francis didn't know how long they'd be able to survive.

Prisoners of the Pole

The mood of the survivors plummeted. Einar Lundborg may have been a thorn in their sides, but his presence ensured an effort by the Swedish government to mount a rescue operation to save him, and with him, the other men. But the small plane had come and gone. Lundborg was gone, but the five men still remained, prisoners of the Pole.

They had no strength left, no hidden untapped sources of energy or confidence. Anger over being left behind sometimes erupted into rage. Biagi would scream at the never-ending horizon, or Cecioni would lash out with his crutch, knocking over a stack of supplies. But more often than not the men sullenly retreated within themselves, afraid to hope or express the desire to escape.

Recently, Alfredo had picked up a transmission from General Nobile that all air landings had been canceled due to the bad weather. No planes could safely land on the badly deteriorating landing strip. Their only hope for survival now would come from the water, the general told him. Several ships from different countries, among them Sweden, Italy, and Russia, would be starting out on an expedition.

"No one's coming," Trojani said weakly. "No one."

"The *Krassin* is already on its way," Alfredo promised the despondent men on the night of July 6. "She can cut through heavy ice floes better than any steamship."

"It can't be too soon," Cecioni loudly complained. "Another few days and we'll all be covered in water."

The mechanic wasn't joking, Alfredo realized. Warmer temperatures had been melting the ice pack at such a fast rate that pools of water spread over the ground and formed small lakes. The men couldn't escape the dampness. They walked in slushy puddles. They ate on the watery ground. Worst of all, they slept in it. All too soon their skin became red and raw and no amount of ointment could cure the sores.

As bad as the ice conditions had become, it couldn't compare to the news that met them on the morning of July 7.

"The *Krassin* can't get to us," a distraught Biagi relayed from the radio. "She's blocked by the ice at Cape North."

A stricken silence greeted his words. *So this is it*, seemed to be the message to the beaten men.

Alfredo got to his feet. He had to bolster their spirits. "It's just a matter of time. The weather is bound to change. We'll hear something positive later this evening."

But they couldn't hear anything. Communication with the *Città* abruptly broke off. For the first time in weeks the men couldn't transmit messages out or pick up the familiar news broadcast from San Paolo in the evening.

Two days passed. The men went through the motions, but their eyes betrayed their state of panic and fear. Alfredo would not succumb to despair. As temporary leader he had to plan for the future. And that future meant keeping his men alive by utilizing whatever equipment and emergency gear was at their disposal.

On July 11, Alfredo ordered the men to stock the small, collapsible boats with food and clothing in case they needed to abandon the unstable ice pack. Once again he had the bundles of food wrapped securely in waterproof canvas, strung together on lines. This way if the boat took on water or capsized, the provisions wouldn't be lost.

"Why are we bothering?" Cecioni said in a despairing voice, watching the men work from the entrance to the tent.

Alfredo was about to reprimand the mechanic, but Francis spoke first.

"We have to continue to have hope," he said. "Hope has brought us this far."

Cecioni snorted. "And you're happy being here, stuck on this rotting watery island of snow and ice?"

Biagi turned from putting on his headphones. "If the general asked me to go with him again to the North Pole, I would do it. For General Nobile."

The words, spoken quietly yet with heartfelt conviction, silenced the men.

Minutes passed as they continued to pack, then Biagi gave a shout.

"It's working again! I've gotten through!"

Everyone turned to the wireless operator.

Biagi scribbled furiously, then looked up, eyes shining.

"The *Krassin*'s on its way! We just need to give our coordinates and location."

The mood of the men instantly brightened. The hours sped by. Alfredo had the men pack their gear in readiness for the evacuation and kept in close communication with General Nobile on the *Città*. On July 12, at 2:55 P.M., they received word to report to the *Città* as soon as they spotted the *Krassin*. The next communication an hour later instructed them to prepare to make smoke signals to alert the Russian icebreaker.

At exactly 4:55 P.M. Alfredo caught sight of the enormous yellow smokestacks high atop the Russian ship.

"I see it! The *Krassin*!" Alfredo shouted.

Everyone cheered. Alfredo's spirits soared and he found it impossible to stop grinning.

"We have sighted the *Krassin* about ten kilometers SW," Biagi transmitted.

But the *Krassin*, unfortunately, had not seen them. The massive ship turned slowly at right angles and began heading north.

A blanket of black despair dropped over the small band. Alfredo kept their spirits up by instructing Biagi to send the *Città* their proper coordinates. The men waited in panicky silence, fear shivering across their faces and twisting their insides.

"Send up smoke signals," the *Krassin* replied.

Trojani worked his smudge fire again at a fevered pitch, aided by Francis. Soon a strong dark pillar of smoke rose in the sky.

At 8:15 A.M. the men heard the piercing shrill of a siren and saw the bow of the icebreaker smash its way through the ice.

"It's coming," Cecioni whispered. Clumsily he wiped one hand across his eyes.

The men huddled together in anticipation, cracking jokes, laughing loudly to disguise their emotional state. Almost forty minutes later the battered old vessel had worked its way to within 150 yards of the now faded Red Tent.

The men stood silently, faces working with emotion, preparing to leave the place where they had been marooned for forty-eight days.

"It's finished?" Francis said. "We're free?" His voice cracked.

Alfredo looked at him, his eyes shining. "Yes, free. Free to return to our homes and families."

At 9:00 P.M. the tireless Biagi tapped out the last message he would send from the ice pack:

"It's over! *Krassin's* here! We're saved!"

The band of tired and dirty men stood up straight, waiting to board the Russian ship with their heads held high. The frozen emptiness of the Arctic hadn't stolen their sanity, or their will to keep going, to live.

Epilogue

The story of the *Italia* disaster did not end with the men's safe return on the *Krassin*. Once the survivors were reunited with their general, they learned that massive rescue attempts had been mounted to save them, organized by eight nations and manned by 1,500 volunteers. Twenty-two airplanes, two dog teams, and as many as fifteen ships played a part in the major undertaking, although sadly, lives were lost among the rescue teams.

Even more devastating was the news of the death of their comrade Finn Malmgren. Although the two senior officers and the Swedish meteorologist had left six weeks before with high hopes and an abundance of rations, the march had deteriorated all too quickly into a disaster.

The men had gone only three days before realizing they were in trouble. Malmgren had to spare his injured shoulder, so his two comrades were forced to carry the extra equipment, food rations, and camp necessities. Marching any distance took longer than expected. At the end of a month Malmgren collapsed, too weakened by frostbite to continue. His friends had to leave him. Torturously Mariano and Zappi crept and stumbled across fields of ice, eventually ending up farther away from their destination than when they had started, owing to the shifting motion of the ice pack. Exhausted and starving, the two men holed up in a six-foot trench, waiting to die. In the third week of June they were shocked but deliriously happy to see planes circling overhead. Zappi laid out strips of rags spelling: HELP FOOD MARIANO ZAPPI and they were finally rescued by the *Krassin* on July 12.

This only added to the aura of failure that clung to the polar expedition. General Nobile returned to Italy a broken man. Although his physical injuries were healing, his emotional state was fragile. Many of his countrymen denounced him as a coward and unfit airship commander. They claimed he caused the *Italia* to crash through faulty and inept directions and then abandoned his men on the ice pack when he was rescued in June. Although his crew members loyally stood by his side, he had to submit to a Commission of Enquiry in February 1929. No formal charges were ever brought against Nobile, and he was never asked to explain his version of the disaster that claimed the lives of seven men. But March 4 newspaper headlines read: "Nobile Blamed for *Italia* Disaster!"

Experts later argued about the reason for the airship's crash. The most likely theory was that ice pellets had punctured the canvas of the outer frame during a storm, releasing large amounts of hydrogen. This, coupled by sudden rises and drops in temperature, made the gas cells expand and then contract, causing the valves to automatically release even more hydrogen, making the ship too heavy. When the *Italia* descended into colder air over the North Pole, she carried so much ice on her frame that she couldn't manage to carry her own weight. A crash would have been inevitable. General Nobile went into semiretirement after the verdict, but returned to his work in airships as a consultant in the Soviet Union, Spain, and eventually the United States. When he died in 1978 at the age of ninety-three, the obituaries called him "the Italian airship designer who had a spectacular career in polar exploration," and "the first person to fly over the North Pole."

Alfredo Viglieri, the young and courageous naval officer, gave untiring service to the Royal Italian Navy during the 1930s and World War II, finally reaching the rank of rear admiral. He remained a steadfast friend of General Nobile all his life.

Francis Behounek, the thirty-one-year-old professor, returned to his homeland, Czechoslovakia, after his rescue, and spent the remainder of his life teaching at the University of Prague. He never went up in a dirigible again.

Perhaps one of the most puzzling questions in this tragic accident concerns the *Italia* and her remaining six crewmen. Where did the airship drift off to? What end did its men meet? No one knows. The mystery of the fate of the airship itself remains unsolved to this day.

Ghost Ship
in the Sky

*The crash of
the British airship
R-101,*

October 5, 1930

On October 5, 1930, all of Britain was in shock and mourning. The country's biggest and most expensive dirigible to rule the skies, the 777-foot R-101, had crashed on its demonstration flight to India. All but six of the fifty-four persons on board the "luxury liner of the air" had died in the fiery crash on a hillside in France.

Two people who were involved with the dirigible in vastly different ways feared the possibility of disaster before the R-101 took off. Twenty-nine-year-old chief engineer Henry Leech helped construct the massive airliner from scratch and knew there were dangerous structural problems that needed to be fixed before the maiden voyage. When he was selected to fly on October 4, he suspected there might be trouble. Another young person who worried about the flight was Eileen Garrett. A gifted psychic and medium, Eileen claimed she saw horrifying visions of the R-101 in flames several years before the actual disaster. Although many scoffed at the psychic craze that was sweeping the nation, others in high places took it seriously. When the renowned creator of Sherlock Holmes, Sir Arthur Conan Doyle, learned of Eileen's terrifying visions, he joined forces with her. Together the world-famous author and medium conducted séances in which they claimed to have received fearful warnings that the R-101 would suffer a tragic fate if it ever took to the skies.

Part ghost story, part documented historical recounting, "Ghost Ship of the Sky" is a true-life drama of one of the most spellbinding aviation crashes in British history.

The Vision

"Hurry," Eileen Garrett pleaded, glancing over her shoulder at her friend. "I can't be late for my appointment."

"You won't be," Julia Cameron said, panting slightly from the strain of trying to keep up. "You aren't meeting James McKenzie for another half hour. Please, Eileen, can't you slow down so I can catch my breath?"

Smiling a little at the sight of Julia's flushed cheeks, Eileen threw up her hands in good-natured surrender. "All right, you win. Let's rest, but only for a minute."

She stopped outside the entrance to Holland Park and sank onto a stone bench. Julia gratefully joined her. It was two o'clock on a sunny March afternoon in London. A feeling of spring was in the air, quite different from the cold wintery days they'd been having, and Eileen felt a similar warming of her own spirits.

The two young women had been hurrying toward the British College of Psychic Science, where they were students. In England in 1928, many famous politicians, writers, and business leaders thought ESP and communication with the dead were not only possible, but probable. Both Julia, twenty-six, and Eileen, thirty-three, took classes in clairvoyance, mental telepathy, and Spiritualism, methods that were supposed to allow the dead to communicate with the living. But it was Eileen who exhibited a real talent in foreseeing the future.

"I still can't believe James McKenzie, the founder himself, wants me to teach some courses at the college," Eileen said with an incredulous smile. "That's why I have this appointment scheduled with him at two-thirty. I can't be late. I have to make the right impression!"

Julia laughed and shook her head. "You *always* make the right impression, Eileen. You're at ease with anyone and anything. That's why we call you 'Queenie.' And let's not forget your amazing gift."

Eileen's smile faded. Sighing, she leaned her head back against the stone bench and wondered if she'd ever overcome her anxiety and fear over her so-called gift. Contrary to what her friends believed, it wasn't always pleasant to receive unexpected visions that were terrifyingly real. There were times when she seriously thought she was mentally ill. Thank goodness James McKenzie understood Eileen and her predicament. Meeting McKenzie and attending his institute had helped her learn to channel her energies, and miraculously stopped the unexpected visions.

"Julia, we should go," she said, checking her watch.

As the two young women stood up, Eileen happened to glance at the sky. A giant airship, brilliant silver in color and over six hundred feet long, emerged from behind a bank of fluffy white clouds and sailed majestically across the park.

Eileen sucked in her breath.

"Look, Julia," she said, gripping her friend's arm. "A dirigible!"

Julia raised her head, shielding her eyes from the sun. "Where? Where's the dirigible?"

"Right above the park gazebo," Eileen said. "You *must* see it. It's huge!"

Julia scanned the sky, then faced Eileen.

"I don't see a thing," Julia said in bewilderment. "Are you sure you aren't mistaking a cloud for an airship?"

"I know a cloud from an airship," Eileen snapped, then immediately felt ashamed. "Julia, I apologize. But I don't understand why you can't see what's directly in front of your eyes . . . Oh, no," Eileen whispered, feeling herself begin to shiver. "I must be having—having a—"

"Vision," Julia concluded. Her eyes sparkled with excitement.

"No," Eileen vehemently denied. "The dirigible is real. Other people must see it."

Julia took her friend's arm. "People don't see it, Eileen. They're walking past, enjoying the park, and not one has called out or pointed upward. You're having a vision."

"No," Eileen murmured. She put a hand to her face as a dull throbbing filled her head. It can't be happening again, she thought. I'll close my eyes, I'll count to three, and when I open them, the dirigible will be gone and I'll be fine.

Leaning against her friend, she squeezed her eyes shut, and then slowly opened them.

The dirigible was still overhead, silently gliding over the tops of the trees in the park. From down below it looked as real as the bandstand gazebo directly in front of them or the buildings in the distance. I'm going crazy, Eileen thought wretchedly. Julia calls it a vision, but I'm hallucinating right here in daylight, in front of all these normal people.

Suddenly, the dirigible wobbled. It pitched forward and barely righted itself again. To Eileen's horror, clouds of black smoke streamed out of the envelope and blurred the control cabin. The dirigible gave a violent shake, then dipped alarmingly toward the ground. As she watched, the airship became lost behind the puffy white clouds. But then she glimpsed billowing masses of fiery black smoke from across the park.

She gripped her hands tightly together. So, it was true. The visions were coming back, despite her lifelong battle to control them.

Orphaned as an infant in Ireland, growing up with a strict, extremely religious aunt and uncle, Eileen had been a sickly, lonely child until her "imaginary playmates" had come to visit her. Always sensitive, she had been devastated when her aunt punished her for telling lies about the friends only she could see. When she experienced her first real vision at the age of ten, she was sent to boarding school in England. "That should drive the demons of lying out of your head," her aunt had sternly said.

Eileen remained in England, and finished her education, happy to escape her critical relatives. But she never was able to escape from the voices and visions that continued to plague her until she met James McKenzie and learned to channel those forces. Now all the progress she had made seemed threatened.

The smoke continued to pour out of the tops of trees.

Even though she knew it was a vision, Eileen couldn't stop herself from trembling.

"What is it?" Julia asked.

"The dirigible just crashed!" Eileen exclaimed. "Oh, Julia, it was so real—and so horrible!"

"But it didn't really happen," Julia assured her. "It's only in your mind."

Eileen bit her lip, worried. "But what if this is something that's going to happen in the future, Julia! Maybe it's not happening now, but it *will*."

Her friend thought for a moment. "I don't believe any dirigibles are flying in Britain right now, although my younger brother who's an aviation nut tells me that the government is currently designing a big luxury aircraft called the R-101. Supposedly the R-101 is going to be as large as the *Titanic*, and just as lavishly furnished. But it will be the safest way to travel throughout the British Empire. It's at least two or three years from completion, though."

"So it's something that *might* occur in the future, when this aircraft is finished," Eileen said in a worried voice.

"Julia, we need to go," Eileen said with unexpected determination. She took a deep breath. "I have to tell James McKenzie about my vision.

Perhaps with his help I can discover *why* the scene of this dirigible crash has come to me, but even more important, what I can do to help prevent the disaster from taking place."

"You're right," Julia confirmed. "James McKenzie will provide an explanation for what's taken place this afternoon. Maybe then you can put your mind at rest."

Eileen didn't respond. She gazed across the park at the billowing mass of dark smoke and felt afraid. Afraid for her own state of mind, but more important, for the men in that deathly dirigible of the future.

The Biggest Airship Ever Built

A prop plane bumpily landed outside the R-101 dirigible hangar some thirty miles from London. The silence of the normally quiet countryside in Cardington was shattered by the whine of the old Handley Page W-8 as it lumbered and jerked down the runway. The unexpected sound brought most of the men working inside the cavernous hangar outdoors to investigate.

Henry Leech was so involved in a wind tunnel experiment, however, that he didn't bother to follow the others. At twenty-eight, Henry, or Harry, as he liked to be called, was one of the youngest foreman engineers of the British Airship Works. He was also one of the most devoted. Harry loved engines with a passion, having grown up assembling (and disassembling) his uncle's motors in the large garage in Surrey. From cars Harry had moved up to planes when he joined the Royal Air Force. All too quickly, however, he realized he'd rather be building airplanes than flying them. And then he was offered the chance of a lifetime: to join forces with the most talented designers and pilots in England to work on the largest dirigible ever constructed.

The R-101, the world's most expensive aircraft to date, was going to be 777 feet long and come in at a cost of almost 1 million dollars. Already newspapers were calling her the "Queen of the Air," the safest way to fly throughout the British Empire. But Germany and America were also racing to put their own dirigibles in the sky first. Harry wanted his country to win the competition, and worked long, grueling hours to make this happen.

"Harry!" one of the mechanics suddenly shouted above the throb of the plane's engines. "You're wanted out on the runway—*now*!"

Harry didn't bother to turn his head. "I can't!" he bellowed impatiently. "I'm in the middle of testing."

"Sir Sefton Brancker wants to see you," the mechanic said in a loud and meaningful voice.

Harry sucked in his breath and straightened.

"What can he want?" Harry's assistant, Alfred Cook, said.

Harry exchanged a nervous glance with Alfred and shook his head. Hurriedly, he wiped the grease from his hands with a rag, then slicked back the reddish-brown hair that constantly fell over his forehead.

"Only one way to find out," he declared, and headed briskly to the hangar entrance.

But his brave words hid a knot of anxiety in his stomach. Whatever Sir Sefton Brancker wanted, it couldn't be good. The last time the air vice marshal had paid a surprise visit to the dirigible hangar, three men had gotten fired and two engineers had been demoted. Harry wasn't even permanently assigned to the R-101. He had been asked to do consulting work on a temporary basis. Had his unconventional suggestions and radical ideas irritated the flight officers so much that they wanted him off the job?

The knot in his stomach grew tighter as he passed his fellow mechanics and engineers. All of them peered at him with worried expressions. Everyone knew Sir Sefton Brancker didn't take time from his hectic schedule to pay meaningless social calls. He was a firecracker of a man, driven by his obsession with completing the R-101 in record time.

Harry held his head up as he marched out of the hangar doors into the blinding March sunlight. No reason to let Sir Brancker or any of the other men think he was afraid. Yet his hands felt slick with perspiration as he approached the plane. Incredibly, the vice marshal, still sitting in the pilot's seat, was motioning for him to climb aboard.

The news must really be grim if he had to be told inside an old prop plane, he thought. Aware that the anxiety in his stomach had now turned into despair, he scrambled up into the copilot's seat of the cramped cockpit.

Sir Brancker eyed him coolly through his monocle.

"Leech," he said without greeting, "word has it that you've been stirring up trouble."

Before Harry could think of a reply, Sir Brancker took the plane down the runway. The engine roared and the body shuddered as it finally lifted off. Harry stared out of the smeared cockpit window at the hangar below.

This is the worst day of my life, he thought miserably. I'm going to be fired 10,000 feet up in the air. To make matters worse, the vice marshal, secretly dubbed "Bad Bump Brancker" by the men, probably wouldn't be able to land the plane smoothly.

"Now then, Leech," Sir Brancker suddenly shouted, "what do you have to say for yourself?"

Harry squeezed his eyes shut in panic as the small-bodied plane dipped in a strong wind and then righted itself.

"I—I don't know what to say, Sir Brancker," Harry began, but was cut off by the vice marshal's brusque bark of a laugh.

"Well, I do," his superior shouted. "I won't have you consulting any longer for us, Leech! I've heard all about your revolutionary ideas for using different engines on the airship. You actually told Commander Colmore that if you were in charge of the project, you'd throw away all the tried-and-true methods of constructing a dirigible and redesign from scratch."

Harry silently groaned. Everything Sir Brancker said was true, but Harry needed to explain the reasons behind his statements. If only Brancker would hear him out, he might get a grasp of the technology Harry wanted to use.

But Sir Brancker wasn't giving him an opportunity to speak. Harry sadly realized that his mind was made up. Nothing Harry would say now would change that.

"Have I made myself clear, Leech?" Brancker snapped.

Harry swallowed his bitter feelings of disappointment and nodded. "I'm no longer going to be doing consulting work on the R-101," he said numbly.

"That's exactly right," Brancker said, then turned and flashed a broad smile at him. "We can't have the newest chief engineer work with us on a temporary basis, you understand. He has to be permanent and full-time. That's right, Leech," Brancker continued, "I want to hire you as the head foreman of the R-101. Whatever you say, goes."

Harry couldn't believe what he was hearing. He wasn't being fired. He was being given a promotion and the chance to be a part of British aviation history. The realization flooded through him with relief and sheer happiness.

Yet even as Sir Brancker turned the plane around to circle the Cardington runway and dirigible hangar, Harry experienced a brief moment of panic. He would be responsible for the success or failure of this venture. The members of the crew would be depending on him.

Airships were prone to being ripped apart by high winds, or exploding in midair for no apparent reason. Would the R-101 be able to withstand these potential dangers and succeed, when so many other dirigibles had failed?

Sir Arthur Conan Doyle on the Case

A drizzle began to fall as they drove out of London. Ten minutes later it turned into a gentle rain that tapped on the roof of the car and blurred the windows. Eileen sat by herself in the backseat, peering out at the gloomy landscape.

What a perfect day for a "ghost hunt," she thought, with a quirk of her lips.

It was the middle of April, almost a month since her vision in Holland Park. James McKenzie and his wife, Doris, had invited Eileen on one of their many ghost-finding expeditions. McKenzie was regularly asked to visit houses that seemed to be haunted. Eileen was so talented at communicating with spirits that McKenzie and his wife often asked her to come along on these trips.

Normally Eileen enjoyed using her abilities to help people, but today she was a little anxious. Maybe her feelings had something to do with the rain that was steadily falling. Or perhaps it had to do with the vision of the dirigible crash that still lingered in her mind. She had listened to James McKenzie when he suggested that the tragedy was something from the *past*, not a premonition as she had feared. "It's most likely a ghostly reenactment of some other airship's going down in another place and time," he tried to assure her. "I guarantee there are others out there with your psychic senses who are receiving the exact same vision."

The words had helped, as had being given a teaching job at the college. For good measure, McKenzie also offered Eileen the use of the building's top floor for "experimental sessions," or sittings. She had a wonderful life, so why was she feeling so strange today?

Something is going to happen out of the ordinary this afternoon, she thought. She just didn't know if it would be good or bad.

James McKenzie carefully navigated a turn onto a narrow side street and glanced back quickly at Eileen.

"We should be there soon," he said. "Feeling all right?"

"Fine." Eileen briefly smiled.

"The woman waiting for us has an interesting story," Doris McKenzie added. "She's recently lost her husband, and both she and her young daughter claim to hear loud rappings coming from within their cottage at all hours. They haven't been able to pinpoint the source and are living in constant fear."

"A poltergeist disturbance is my guess," James said. "But you'll be able to tell us what's happening with more certainty."

Eileen nodded, eager to reach the house and find out what was in store for her.

"This is the address," Doris announced, as her husband pulled over in front of a small cottage.

Eileen stared out the window. "Who's that man standing outside the front door? Is someone else joining us?"

James helped his wife from the car, then came to open Eileen's door. "I think you'll be pleasantly surprised by this mystery guest."

Eileen followed the McKenzies up the walk to the front door and then stopped when the stranger turned to greet them. The big, bearlike man with the thick walrus mustache, twinkling blue eyes, and shrewdly animated features was well known to her, even without having been introduced. Everyone in England knew the famed creator of the brilliant detective Sherlock Holmes—Sir Arthur Conan Doyle.

The author, in his late sixties, had once fiercely declared Spiritualism "as the greatest nonsense on earth." But James had told Eileen that Sir Arthur had slowly changed his outlook. He now believed whole-heartedly in life after death and the validity of psychic research. So much so that a large portion of the public called Sir Arthur ridiculous and deluded. Criticism didn't seem to bother him, though. The only thing that did matter was proving that souls exist independent of their bodies and that spirits can communicate with the living.

"Sir Arthur," James said warmly, "how wonderful it is that you could join us."

Eileen watched James shake the burly author's hand, then Doris added her own greeting.

Eileen found herself being led over to Sir Arthur Conan Doyle, who was regarding her with intense interest from under thick white eyebrows.

"Miss Eileen Garrett," James McKenzie said, "may I present Sir Arthur Conan Doyle?"

"How do you do," Eileen said, and hesitated. "I've heard so much about you, sir, and I've read and enjoyed all your books."

Sir Arthur shook her extended hand and then bowed. "And I, too, have heard so much about you, Miss Garrett. Your reputation as a medium and psychic precedes you."

Flustered, Eileen peered across at James, who gave her an encouraging smile.

"Sir Arthur has expressed an interest in sitting on an advisory council at the college," James explained. "He believes the work we've been doing can only help further the cause of psychic research."

"Your own capabilities in this area have led me to join you this afternoon," Sir Arthur said. His bright blue eyes were sharp and alert as he held Eileen's gaze. "You see, Miss Garrett, I had a second reason for wanting to attend this poltergeist investigation. There is a favor I must ask of you and I hope you will hear me out with an open mind."

Eileen felt her breath catch. Whatever could England's most celebrated detective writer want from her? Steady, she told herself firmly. Don't get all flustered. Yet she could feel her heart begin to pound under Sir Arthur's intense yet kindly scrutiny.

Before she could think of a reply, the soft drizzle turned into a harder, driving rain.

"Let's get out of this terrible weather," Doris said, and knocked on the cottage door. The door was opened by a thin-faced woman in her early thirties, clutching the hand of a frail-looking little girl by her side.

Even before introductions were made, Eileen could sense a disturbing presence inside the house. She was so gripped by the sensation that she barely heard Sir Arthur whisper, "We will talk after the session."

It was always this way. Whenever Eileen felt the presence of a spirit, her skin began to prickle and her back began to ache, yet once she actually *saw* the spirit the unpleasant feelings disappeared. Now an hour and a half passed in a blur as the four "ghost-hunters" first investigated the source of the unexplained raps, then James put Eileen in a trance. The two had worked together so long that the hypnotic trance took only minutes to bring about. Eileen sat back in a comfortable chair and closed her eyes as James spoke softly to her, urging her to let go of all her conscious thought by imagining a stream. Within minutes Eileen's head dropped as she went into a sleeplike state. It was at this moment that the spirit of the recently deceased father of the little girl came through. He had been knocking, he fiercely declared through Eileen's voice, to make his family aware that he resented the squandering of their inheritance and to assure his daughter that he still loved her.

When the session was over, Eileen slowly awakened, stretching her tight shoulder blades and yawning. Opening her eyes, she stared up at the ring of faces peering at her.

"Did anything happen?" she asked.

"Real contact has been made today," James stated. "We've discovered the source of the rapping and hopefully put an end to it."

"Astounding," Sir Arthur declared. He stood in the corner, regarding Eileen with open admiration. "She truly has the gift."

James explained to Eileen what had transpired while she was in the trance as Doris comforted the obviously shaken widow and little girl. Sir Arthur took it all in, those shrewd blue eyes never leaving Eileen's face.

When Eileen slowly stood, Sir Arthur was immediately at her side. "Perhaps now we can continue our conversation, Miss Garrett?"

Eileen nodded.

"Now then," he began, "I wonder if you could help me, and in so doing, perhaps help England as well."

"Help England?" Eileen echoed in surprise.

"I am gravely concerned about a matter that's come to my attention. A Mrs. Beatrice Earl has written to me about receiving messages from a pilot whose plane has recently disappeared over the Atlantic. Mrs. Earl believes that the pilot has died and is desperately attempting to communicate with his family and friends."

"And you are requesting that I conduct a sitting with this woman, Mrs. Earl?" Eileen said. "But how is this a matter of urgency for England?"

"Mrs. Earl revealed in her letter that the pilot

needed to contact a friend of his, the navigator on an airship the government is building called the R-101."

"An airship?" Eileen froze at the statement. "What—what was the message?"

Sir Arthur stroked his walrus mustache and frowned. "I fear it is the very worst kind. The pilot claims to have intimate knowledge of this airship and believes that disaster will result if the R-101 is put into operation."

Eileen felt an immediate chill. Here was another warning of a dirigible in danger. Was it meant for the same dirigible she had seen over Holland Park?

"What can I do to help, Sir Arthur?" she said. "I am afraid that I've also received visions of a dirigible in trouble, a dirigible that crashes into flames and smoke."

"Will you meet with Beatrice Earl and the wife of this missing pilot if I arrange it?"

Eileen quickly nodded. "At their earliest convenience. I'll be glad to help in any way I can to prevent a terrible tragedy from occurring."

Sir Arthur regarded her gravely, then took her hand. "I sense the two of us are embarking on serious business, one that may jeopardize our reputations. May God be with us both."

And with the men of that doomed dirigible, Eileen silently added. I pray we're not too late.

First Trial Flight

"Hey, wake up, Chief," someone said loudly. "Time to get moving."

Harry groaned and cracked open an eyelid to find one of his engineers, Jim, staring down at him.

"What time is it? Where am I?' he groggily mumbled.

"It's nearly seven in the morning," Jim said. "You worked so late in the hangar last night that you slept on the sofa in the administration building."

"Again?" Harry said. He rubbed his eyes, then sat up with a jerk.

"Today's November sixteenth!" he exclaimed. "Members of the British Parliament are coming on board the R-101 for a short trial flight and I'm wasting precious time sacked out on this sofa." He jumped up and looked out the windows of the office. Dark, heavy clouds covered what little could be seen of the morning sun. "I don't like these clouds," he muttered.

"There's a strong wind kicking up, as well," Jim added. "If the weather gets any worse, I wouldn't advise taking our baby out for a trial spin."

"Of all the rotten luck," Harry said, now fully awake and anxious to get back to work. "Have you gotten word yet about the conditions of the gas cells? We loosened the wire netting around them to enlarge their capacity, but I've heard reports that the cells are rubbing against the metal frame of the airship and are ripping."

"I'll check on that," Jim promised, then frowned. "If the cells are losing gas, that's a big problem."

"Make sure you find out if the expanding cells are swinging back and forth too freely in the hull, as well. Motion like that could make the ship unstable and cause it to go into sudden, deep dives."

"Will do, Chief," Jim said, and exited quickly.

Harry gazed across at the hangar. He didn't want to worry about the R-101. It had tested so well over the last several months. But he couldn't ignore important problems. He was the head engineer and took his job seriously. He had to rule out any possibility of danger before permitting the aircraft to take off.

Slicking back his rumpled hair, Harry left the administration building to head for the hangar. There was important work to be done before the seventy-two members of Parliament arrived.

Six hours later Harry waited nervously in the still gloomy, overcast afternoon to greet the members of Parliament. He and the other officers of the Royal Airship Works stood outside the huge hangar at the base of the mooring mast. Nearly two hundred feet above their heads the R-101 rolled in the increasing winds. One end of the airship was firmly gripped by mooring cables at the very top of the stout, triangular steel tower, so there was little chance the dirigible could break away. To board the R-101, passengers would be whisked up in an elevator inside the mooring tower to a catwalk that led into the ship.

The tension level was growing among the officers and crew of the R-101 as the members of Parliament pulled up in taxis and private cars. Small clusters of spectators, as well as newspaper reporters, lined up behind the police barriers surrounding the mooring tower.

Harry listened to the sound the the R-101's giant diesel engines made. Beside him, his good friend and assistant engineer, Alfred Cook, shot him a worried look.

"Sound all right to you, Alfred?" Harry said in a low voice.

The assistant engineer didn't need to ask what Harry meant. Potentially the most dangerous feature of the ship, the five diesel engines inside the R-101 were not like any other gasoline engine found on airships before. Called Beardmore Tornadoes, the R-101 engines were originally designed for Canadian railway locomotives. They weighed 4,700 pounds each and seventeen tons total. The heavy pieces of machinery were attached to the underside of the dirigible in five little power cars. Privately Harry joked to his men that they resembled toy cars at some amusement park ride.

But this was not a laughing matter today. With the MPs aboard for a trial flight over the English Channel, all eyes would be fixed on the success—or failure—of this test of the R-101's airworthiness. Much of that success would reflect on Harry, so he mentally kept his fingers crossed that his men had worked out any kinks in the big diesel engines.

Beside him, Alfred concentrated on the sound of the throbbing engines. Finally he smiled nervously.

"They're performing up to speed, Chief," he said. "No cause for alarm."

Harry grunted. Just a month ago the R-101 had been taken for a thirteen-hour flight over the English Channel. The engines had sounded fine then, too. But three engines had failed during the flight. The aluminum pipes of the cooling system had cracked and had to be replaced by rubber hoses in midair before the engines could be restarted. Much as Harry didn't like to admit it, there was always something breaking down on the R-101. It was almost as if the airship were cursed.

"Chief, look," Alfred murmured. "Lord Thomson's arriving."

Harry and all the men of the Royal Airship Works straightened. Lord Thomson was the secretary of state for air, a tall, aloof man who regarded the R-101 as his personal creation and brainchild. Everyone knew that Lord Thomson had his eye on becoming the viceroy of India, the British Empire's most prestigious post. It was because of this ambition that Lord Thomson had begun pushing for the maiden voyage of the R-101 to India.

Harry hoped that the secretary of state wasn't going to make any surprise announcements about the scheduling of the official first flight. There was still too much work to be done on the airship. The crowd began edging closer to Lord Thomson, sensing an announcement. Even the members of Parliament who had been giving statements to the various reporters now fell silent.

Major George Scott, the commander in charge of airship flights, moved to stand in front of Harry. Squad Leader Ernest Johnston, the R-101's chief navigator, accompanied him. Judging from the tight-lipped expressions on both men's faces, Harry guessed there was trouble ahead. Sure enough, Lord Thomson brought up the topic of the maiden voyage to India almost immediately. To Harry's shock, the secretary of state offered a firm date of the proposed first flight: "September of 1930, at the latest."

"Has he gone completely mad?" Major Scott muttered angrily to Johnston. "That gives us less than a year for more testing! That's not enough time to let us know if the R-101 can survive in tropical storms on the long passage to India."

"And what if there's an emergency over the Atlantic, or the Indian Ocean?" Johnston said with a worried frown. "Or the Sahara, for that matter? Ten months for more trial runs is sheer madness!"

Harry had been startled to hear his private fears voiced aloud by the two officers in charge of the airship. If they felt this strongly about more testing of the R-101, couldn't they persuade Lord Thomson to postpone his long flight to India, or at least alter the route to make it shorter and safer?

One thing was certain: If Lord Thomson got his way, Harry couldn't predict what the R-101 would do on this long and potentially dangerous maiden voyage.

A Séance

While Lord Thomson was announcing the date for his trip to India, Eileen was meeting Mrs. Beatrice Earl and the wife of the missing pilot. It had taken many months to coordinate the experimental session. Sir Arthur had left unexpectedly for a lecture tour right after the ghost-hunting expedition, and Mrs. Earl had been abroad. However, Eileen had persisted in her letters to Mrs. Earl and was rewarded by having these two guests finally knocking on the door of the college's top-floor suite.

First-time visitors to the sitting room were pleasantly surprised by its cheerful, cozy atmosphere. On this damp November afternoon, a fire crackled merrily in the grate as Eileen welcomed her guests.

Mrs. Beatrice Earl was an elderly, respectable-looking woman. She hovered just inside the sitting room door with a sheepish expression on her face. Holding on to her arm was a woman almost thirty years younger, dark-haired, pretty, with flushed cheeks and a hopeful yet frightened look on her face. Eileen was familiar with that look. So many of her clients came to her in despair or disbelief, feeling foolish about consulting a medium but wanting desperately to confirm that their deceased loved ones were still alive in some way.

Eileen didn't know at this point whether the young woman's husband had indeed died in the plane crash or was still alive. She would approach the sitting with an open mind and hope the results would not prove too devastating for either of her visitors.

"I am Eileen Garrett," she introduced herself with a reassuring smile. She reached out and shook the older woman's hand. "And you must be Beatrice Earl. Please, won't you both come inside and make yourselves comfortable by the fire?"

At all her sessions Eileen refused to hear anything about those seeking her help. She felt that a blank slate guaranteed legitimate results. So she did not ask the younger woman anything about herself. She warmly smiled at her, however, and took her heavy coat. When both women were seated comfortably, Eileen explained that she had something called a "guide" or a "control." After she went into a trance, the voice of the control would speak through her. Eileen would be merely a channel with no control over what was being said.

"Will we see or feel *anything* during the session?" Beatrice Earl asked.

"If any presence does make itself felt," Eileen hastened to assure her, "it will be solely through my voice."

The younger woman hesitated, then reached into her handbag. Smiling uncertainly, she took out a pencil and a notebook. "Would you mind if I record the session today? I'm fairly well-versed in stenography skills."

Eileen laughed. "Delighted. I wish I could hire you to transcribe *all* of my sittings. Now then, are you both quite ready?"

The two women exchanged nervous glances, then the younger one nodded. She poised the pencil above the notebook and waited.

Eileen shut her eyes and began to breathe deeply. One minute she was sitting upright in her chair, aware of the ticking of a clock in the room and the sounds of traffic outside. The next she was slipping into a trance. Sometimes she was conscious of the different voices coming out of her mouth, other times not. Today she was half-awake and able to hear herself during the session.

It was a strange sensation; she could hear herself talking but she couldn't control any of her movements. She leaned in the direction of the young woman. Her mouth opened.

"You are a newcomer," she heard herself say in a voice that wasn't her own. "You have never been here before."

Someone gasped and then silence fell. The voice continued.

"A young man comes to you. He went out suddenly. He was a pilot and full of life."

For the next five minutes the voice went on, giving details of the identity of the man whose spirit was present in the room.

Eileen found herself slowly tuning out, going into that blankness similar to sleep.

When she slowly came to, she found her client crying softly.

"He has passed over," the young widow said. "Now I know for certain that my husband is dead. Raymond came to me. I can swear to it. There were so many things about me and our life together that only he could know."

Mrs. Earl nodded, then raised a troubled face to Eileen. "The notes my friend took down include a warning of great importance. The same warning that I received. It must be passed on."

"Who is the warning to?' Eileen asked.

The young woman frowned. "An airman friend of my husband's, I believe, a man called Ernest Johnston, or Johnny. He is a navigational officer involved in the R-101 project, and Raymond made it very clear that he needed to get word to him."

Eileen's expression didn't change but she felt a sudden sick feeling in her stomach. Here was the third warning about a dirigible.

Regaining her composure, Eileen asked the widow for the exact message that her deceased husband wanted to pass on to the navigator working on the R-101.

The woman wiped away her tears and opened her notebook.

"'Johnston must listen,'" she read. "'From what I know, the whole idea of dirigibles is spending money in vain, for they are not practical. Johnston thinks the airship is all right, but I have serious concerns about it. I'm afraid they're rushing things.'" She paused, her voice trembling. "'Even if nothing happens on the maiden voyage, she is not going to last. *There will be an accident.*'"

Here were names and facts Eileen could verify. Without showing her anxiety, Eileen made the women tea and then excused herself. Hurrying into an office down the hall, she closed the door and called Sir Arthur. He knew about the scheduled session and picked up on the first ring.

"What happened?" he immediately enquired.

"I'm afraid it's not good," Eileen said. "The

missing pilot is dead and has confirmed what we feared, that there's going to be trouble with the R-101 if it's ever put in flight. But now we have names and facts to verify the findings."

Eileen proceeded to relay the exact words of the deceased pilot and the name of the airship's navigator.

There was silence on the other end as Sir Arthur digested this information. Eileen could almost picture the writer deliberating over the next course of action, his intense blue eyes narrowed, one hand stroking the thick walrus mustache. When he finally spoke, his voice was firm and commanding.

"The time has come to bring this to Sir Sefton Brancker's attention. Brancker is the director of civil aviation. I can't promise that he'll believe me or will want to see you, but at least we'll have tried."

"In the interim, is there anything further I can do?" Eileen asked.

Sir Arthur sighed. "You've done a great deal already, but please be open to seeing Mrs. Earl and the young widow again. It's essential that we sustain the contact you've made with this pilot fellow and add any new information about the inherent dangers of the R-101."

"I'll gladly do that," Eileen assured him. "I'll do anything to prevent that terrifying vision from coming true. But I'm afraid that time is running out."

"The R-101 Must Fly!"

"Did any of you see today's headlines?" Sir Arthur stood in the entrance to Eileen's sitting room, clutching a rolled-up newspaper in his hand. "It says that the R-101 and the German dirigible, the *Graf Zeppelin*, are in a race to be the first to launch a round-the-world flight. They've even set a date for the R-101's maiden voyage to India: September of this year!"

"Oh, no," Eileen said, quickly scanning the front page that Sir Arthur held out to her. "That doesn't leave us much time!"

Beatrice Earl and Emilie Hinchcliffe, the widow of the deceased pilot Raymond Hinchcliffe, were paying a social call on Eileen. The three women had been become good friends since the first sittings in November, six months before. Together with Sir Arthur, they often met at the British College of Psychic Science to conduct sittings. During these sessions, warnings continued to come through about the dangers of the R-101.

"I've met twice now with Ernest Johnston," Emilie Hinchcliffe said, as Sir Arthur joined them before the fire. "But he simply won't listen when I pass on the warnings from my husband. He thanks me for my time and effort, but tells me my concerns are misplaced." Emilie gazed helplessly at her friends. "What else can we do?"

Sir Arthur drummed his fingers impatiently on the arm of the sofa.

"We must not give up. I'll ring Sir Brancker again."

Months passed and work continued on the R-101. One afternoon Eileen was walking her dog in London's Hyde Park. Once again she happened to look up. The great silver ship sailed smoothly overhead until it wobbled, gave a sharp lurch, then began spewing black smoke from its envelope. The ship nosed down until it disappeared behind some buildings. That made three visions of disaster. Eileen stood trembling, sickened by the certainty that the R-101 would crash, but powerless to prevent the tragedy.

"I have to do *something*," she vowed softly. "I have to try to warn someone on my own."

She got her chance in mid-September, less than

two weeks before the ship was to take off. She attended a party where a close friend, Auriol Lee, was also a guest. Auriol was a renowned stage actress as well as a longtime friend of Sir Sefton Brancker. When Eileen heard this she quietly pulled the actress aside and revealed her concerns about the R-101.

"Perhaps you could speak to Sir Brancker for me," Eileen said. "It's urgent that he stop this aircraft from flying."

Auriol listened in silence, then gestured for Eileen to follow her. Eileen was led through a crowded sitting room until Auriol came to an abrupt halt in front of two men. The shorter man exclaimed joyously upon seeing the actress, "My dear Auriol! I had no idea you'd be here this evening."

The two exchanged warm greetings, then Auriol tactfully pulled him away from the other guest.

"Sir Sefton Brancker," Auriol said, "may I present my good friend Eileen Garrett."

Eileen gazed wordlessly at the director of civil aviation. It was a fateful—or simply lucky—meeting, but would Sir Sefton listen to what she had to say?

"I'll leave you two alone to talk," Auriol said, then gave Eileen an encouraging nod before she melted into the crowd.

"Now then," Sir Sefton said with a nervous laugh, "are you the psychic lady Sir Arthur Conan

Doyle keeps asking me to meet?"

"Yes, I am," Eileen replied more bravely than she felt. She took a deep breath and proceeded to recount in detail all the visions and messages she had received in the last year and a half about the R-101.

During her detailed explanation, Sir Sefton played with his monocle, his face revealing polite, if strained, interest.

"You realize, young lady, that I'm planning on flying to India on that very same aircraft in the next two weeks. I hope you are just daydreaming about what has already happened. You see, I'm committed to flying with Lord Thomson and the others."

Eileen gravely shook her head. "I wish I felt the same as you, but I don't. Isn't there any way that the flight can be canceled?"

"We are committed," Sir Sefton replied forcefully. "The R-101 must fly!"

His eyes betrayed a sudden uneasiness, but he cut off Eileen's continued protests with a polite but firm silencing hand.

"Then I can only offer my heartfelt prayers that your trip will be a success," Eileen said sadly.

Shoulders slumping, she excused herself to find Auriol Lee. She had tried, but she had failed. The R-101 was planning its maiden voyage in less than two weeks, and nothing—and no one—could stop it.

The Journey Begins

At five o'clock in the afternoon on October 4, 1930, Harry drove his car slowly around the crowds of people gathered at the mooring tower at Cardington. His wife, Clare, sat nervously beside him. The day of reckoning had finally arrived. The R-101 was scheduled to make history by traveling to India in less than six days, an unheard-of achievement in air travel.

But is she really ready to undertake the long voyage? Harry worried privately. So much depended on the last-minute repairs he and his men had made on the troublesome diesel engines. Just three days before, the air cooler of one engine had failed during a short test flight. Harry had spent all night working under the glare of floodlights to correct the problem. He was hopeful the rest of the Beardmore Tornadoes would operate smoothly. But a fragile thing like hope wouldn't account for much once the big dirigible was flying over the dangerous waters of the English Channel.

Clare peered out the window of the car.

"It looks like the dark clouds overhead aren't going away," she said in a tense voice. "Surely they'll cancel the flight if it starts to rain."

"The flight won't be canceled," Harry told her. "Lord Thomson is insistent that he leave England today so he can attend a political meeting in India on October tenth."

"But if he knows there's bad weather ahead, surely he won't risk his life—and your life, too—to make some foolish deadline!"

Harry didn't respond. He concentrated on pulling into the special parking area reserved for passengers and flight members behind the mooring tower. He couldn't tell his wife another worrisome fact: the meteorologist named Giblett had already called to let him know that a storm was predicted over the Channel and supposed to be hitting northern France by 8 P.M. Winds could reach twenty to thirty miles an hour. Clouds would drop down to about 1,000 feet, severly reducing visibility.

Clare pinned a sprig of white heather onto Harry's jacket lapel after they got out of the car.

"For luck," she whispered, then burrowed her face against his shoulder. "I wish you weren't going."

"I *have* to go," he said, hugging her. "These are *my* engines on the ship, and I can be of help if anything goes wrong."

Clare shuddered, and Harry quickly added, "But nothing is going to happen. Besides, Major Scott and Johnston would never agree to take off if they had any doubts at all about the airworthiness of the ship."

Gripping his suitcase in hand, Harry led Clare through the crowd of the officers' wives and families at the base of the tower. Most of the fifty-four passengers on the flight were officers and crew, with only six invited official guests, among them Lord Thomson and his valet. Harry had been asked to go as a civilian guest as well, in thanks for all his years of work on the airship. It was an honor of a lifetime, he realized. He felt a tingle of anticipation and pride when he glanced up at the dirigible, swaying two hundred feet above them in the gusty winds. Spotlights positioned on the ground brilliantly illuminated the colossal silvery hull. Under the darkening leaden layer of clouds, the R-101 rolled above them like a shimmering ghost. Lights twinkled inside the five small power cars and from the dining lounge above the control cabin.

Clare fought back tears as she embraced Harry in a final farewell, then lightly touched the sprig of heather in his buttonhole.

"Think of me," she said softly.

"Always," Harry replied. He winked at her. "But I'll be back before you even miss me."

With a final wave, Harry turned and pushed past the crowd of reporters to enter the base of the tower. Already several officers were waiting impatiently for the freight-sized elevator.

Harry greeted Major Scott and Sir Sefton Brancker. He couldn't help noticing how grim their faces were. Rumors had been circulating around the hangar that Sir Brancker had been talking to psychics about the chances of success for the upcoming flight. The senior staff members had scoffed at this nonsense, but Harry had privately overheard a conversation between Sir Brancker and Major Scott that sounded as if Brancker was suddenly requesting a postponement of the scheduled air date. Perhaps the psychic rumor hadn't been so ridiculous, he thought.

Just then the elevator clanged to a stop on the bottom level and Lord Thomson hurried into the tower.

"Hold that elevator!" he demanded.

Harry was shocked by the number of suitcases and personal belongings Lord Thomson had with him. Even worse was the plush and heavy-looking red carpet his valet carried over his arm. Each passenger was instructed to bring ten pounds or less of luggage. Any more than that and the balance and stability of the R-101 could be affected.

Major Scott's jaw dropped at Lord Thomson's flouting of the rules. But it was his superior, Sir Brancker, who dared speak his mind.

"As you're well aware, Lord Thomson, we've had ongoing problems with this aircraft, and for you to add this unneccessary weight is not only foolhardy and selfish, but *dangerous*."

Lord Thomson's face flushed with anger. "How can you question the airworthiness of the R-101? I've heard all your irritating and unfounded concerns before, but I won't be badgered into changing my plans now!"

Sir Brancker leaned forward, his soft words an urgent plea. "I've warned you before, the ship is not fit to go. *Face the facts and call off this flight*."

Lord Thomson's eyes narrowed. "All right, if *you* are afraid to go—don't! There are many others who would jump at the chance!"

In the shocked silence that followed, Lord Thomson swept into the waiting elevator, followed by his valet and assistants. The doors clanged shut and the elevator began to rise.

Harry stared at Major Scott in stunned amazement. He should not have been present to overhear this conversation. If Sir Brancker felt the airship should not take off, why were they going ahead with the flight?

As if sensing his confusion and distress, Major Scott rested a hand on Harry's shoulder. "It's all right," he said with conviction. "I'm in command and nothing will happen to us."

Thirty miles away in London, Eileen was undergoing another session with Emilie Hinchcliffe. At 6:36 P.M., when the R-101 left Cardington for her historic trip to India, a spirit message came through from Captain Raymond Hinchcliffe concerning the dirigible. It was brief but all too clear: "Storms rising. Nothing but a miracle can save them."

"An Engine Has Stopped!"

The weather was getting worse.

Harry sipped his coffee and watched the empty saucer rattle on the table. From the observation windows of the elegant dining room, he could see rain slashing against the glass. The lights of the small towns and farmhouses below gleamed up at them in the dark like miniature diamonds.

The others sitting down to dinner had not commented on the storm, or on the gradual pitching and rolling of the ship. Perhaps the officers were used to far worse, and this rolling seemed of minor importance. Perhaps the six dignitaries at the table had such faith in this highly regarded "luxury liner of the sky" that any thought of possible disaster didn't occur to them.

Certainly Major Scott's expression gave nothing away, Harry noted. The officer had taken time to join them in the dining room and behaved as if there were nothing wrong.

Harry finished his dessert of rice custard and reached for a piece of fruit from a serving bowl. The ship made another jolting motion. The crystal bowl slid a few inches from his outstretched hand. This *couldn't* be normal for a craft of her weight and power. Surely the R-101 should be maintaining a more stable flight path? Across the table, Squadron Leader Rope, the assistant to the ship's designer, caught his eye.

"I never knew her to roll so much," Rope said in a private aside to Harry. "She feels more like a seagoing ship than an aircraft."

But Rope smiled wryly at his own comment. He wasn't concerned about the ship. It was the first time Harry had been up in any kind of rough weather, so maybe this rocking motion was to be expected. He sighed and patted the sprig of heather on his jacket. He would sit back and enjoy the elegant surroundings as he finished dinner.

Harry smiled as he surveyed the room. Spending most of his time in the belly of the ship, he couldn't quite get over the deluxe accommodations for the paying passengers. There were two separate decks for those flying in style. The upper level consisted of the private sleeping quarters, the dining room, and a lounge extending thirty-two by sixty feet between glassed-in promenade decks. The lower level boasted an elegant smoking room, bathrooms, and an observation galley. The R-101 had been advertised as a skyliner, and the white-and-gold trim of the quarters, complemented by the polished wood and Persian carpets on the floors, resembled a first-class hotel.

Harry finished his coffee and a white-jacketed steward promptly appeared at his side, offering to pour him a fresh cup. Yes, he marveled, everything about the ship was of the highest quality, from the service to the linen tablecloth and gleaming silverware, to the tastefully arranged floral centerpieces. There had even been the most expensive champagne to toast the historic occasion.

When Rope suggested they head for the smoking room on the lower level after dinner, Harry readily agreed. A drink of tonic water and lime would hit the spot right now—and also help calm his nerves. The R-101 had traveled barely thirty-five miles and seemed to be fighting the gusting winds and heavy rain. As Harry sank into the wicker sofa in the lounge, he couldn't help but wonder how his engines were holding up.

"I just heard a revised forecast from the control room," Rope confided. "Unfortunately, winds have picked up to forty to fifty miles per hour. That means our ground speed will be reduced ten to twenty miles per hour. It's going to delay us."

Harry caught his breath at this news. "Winds are that strong?"

Rope hesitated, then shrugged his shoulders. "Yes, but I have every faith she'll be up to the challenge."

They had been in the air less than an hour when Arthur Bell, the engineer in the aft-engine power car, popped his head into the lounge.

Harry took one look at Bell's face and knew something was wrong.

"It's the main oil pressure, sir," Bell informed Harry. "An engine has stopped!"

Harry was on his feet in seconds. "I'll be right there," he said.

As he headed to the power car, he patted the sprig of heather.

A Low Ship
Over London

Eileen bowed her head under the weight of the winds and rain and quickened her steps. All around her people were hurrying along the streets, gazing upward at the stormy skies. Others stood on building rooftops or leaned out of windows, enduring the chilly wind and rain to catch a glimpse of the R-101 as she sailed over London.

The airship would be flying over the city at approximately 8:30 P.M., but Eileen had left her apartment fifteen minutes earlier in order not to miss the sight. What am I doing out here? she wondered, not for the first time. Why did I cancel dinner plans with friends to hurry along crowded streets in a downpour? But she knew the answer. She had to witness the dirigible flying overhead for herself. She had to see the *real* dirigible, not the horrifying one in her visions.

And she was doing it, not only for herself, but in

honor of Sir Arthur. He had died from a heart attack only a short time before. All of England mourned the passing of the great writer, but none more than his close friends.

Eileen greatly missed his keen intellect and his interest in psychic matters. The two had developed a close friendship over the last two years.

Up until the very end, Sir Arthur had been pressuring the British Air Ministry to postpone the airship's maiden voyage. Nothing had managed to stop the airship from taking off, but now she could witness its flight as it soared over London. Hopefully Sir Arthur's spirit would be with her.

Suddenly someone beside her drew in an excited breath and shouted, "I see it!"

Everyone on the street stopped and craned their necks. Eileen looked up and saw the giant silver ship slowly circle Westminster and begin to move down the Thames. From below it resembled a miniature floating city, ablaze with twinkling lights. She couldn't hear the engines above the sound of city traffic, but steamships and tugs tooted and blew their horns to greet the ship. Parents standing in front of Eileen picked up their children and told them to wave their handkerchiefs.

"This is British aviation history," a proud father was telling his two young sons.

Eileen suddenly froze. Just as in her vision the dirigible was dipping, then rising. Her nose was pointing down, her tail up. A chill deeper than the rainy cold went straight through her.

"She's awfully low," someone whispered.

The R-101 had dipped so close to the tower of Big Ben that it looked like she was going to hit the top. But at the very last minute, the aircraft pulled itself up.

I can't believe this, Eileen thought in horror. The dirigible was jerking and twisting like a child's balloon in a strong wind. All around her uneasy murmuring broke out.

She stared into the illuminated windows along the observation galley of the airship. It was so low she could easily make out the faces of passengers peering down at the crowds. They were smiling, some waving. No one appeared particularly worried or frightened.

But they should be, Eileen thought, with sickening certainty.

Before the night was out the R-101 was going to crash, all her senses told her.

Ignoring the rain pelting her upturned face, she continued to follow the erratic path of the dirigible as it moved out of sight.

A Storm Warning
Over the Channel

The R-101 crossed the English Channel at 9:35 P.M.

The weather had gotten worse as the airship flew over the dark, windswept sea. Rain slashed against the sides of the ship and collected on top of the hull, making her top-heavy and hard to navigate.

From his cramped space in the aft-engine gondola, Harry paused for a moment to peer out the window. He was shocked to see how low the ship was sailing. Even in the darkness he could make out the choppy white waves. He estimated that the R-101 was only six hundred to seven hundred feet above the water. Judging from the thrust of the winds and the increased fury of the rain, Harry sensed they were flying directly toward the center of a rising storm.

The captain must know what he is doing, he thought. Major Scott had every belief in the safety and reliability of his aircraft, and that's why he had chosen not to turn around and head back to Cardington. They were going on—toward Paris. At least four of the five diesel engines were operating at full speed, but Harry still couldn't get the stubborn aft engine to respond. The useless machine added nearly five thousand pounds to the already heavy airship.

The three engineers worked for another hour inside the tiny gondola. Finally they got the problem engine going again around ten-thirty.

"Success at last," Arthur Bell cried triumphantly.

"Just be sure to keep a sharp eye out," Harry warned. "It may cause trouble again."

Harry gave his cramped back muscles a stretch and wearily climbed the ladder up to the passengers' top level. I need a rest, he thought, heading for his stateroom. He entered his small but elegantly quarters and lay down on the bunk. An hour or so later he was still awake. The rolling and pitching of the ship, as well as anxiety over the engines, prevented him from sleeping. With a sigh, he got up.

The passenger decks were quiet as Harry made his way back to the smoking room. The overhead lights had been dimmed. Judging from the snores coming from the cabins, most of the passengers were sleeping soundly. He should be asleep, too, he told himself, but it was no use. Excitement and nervous tension kept him wide-awake.

Once again he entered the lounge. Only Chief Engineer Gent occupied the spacious room, and Harry joined him.

"I've managed to get all engines up and running," Harry reported, "but I don't know for how long. Quite frankly I'm worried about them. And I don't like the way the ship's rolling and pitching so violently."

"It's a bad night and we've had some problems," Gent replied. "But we'll get through it fine."

Moments later Captain Irwin, Major Scott's second-in-command, dropped in to take a break.

"The aft engine's settled down and running smoothly," he assured both men. "We've just crossed the French coast and God willing, should be flying out of the storm in another fifty miles."

Bidding them a good evening, Captain Irwin left the two engineers to return to the control cabin.

"There, you see," Gent said with a relieved grin, "there's nothing to worry about. I'm beat and off to bed."

And with a yawn and final good-night, he took leave of Harry.

Harry remained in the wicker chair, tapping nervous fingers against the arm rest. Flying over the Channel was relatively safe. The airship could dive and pitch without fear of hitting anything. But once they were headed over the mountainous countryside of France, any sharp dip could result in the ship's striking land or a building. Harry felt himself go cold as he imagined the consequences of such an event.

He couldn't sit still any longer. Despite the late hour, he felt compelled to make a check of all five engine cars.

Somebody screamed.

Eileen jerked awake and listened in the darkness, tense and shaken. But there was no other outcry. There was nothing but silence.

But she had heard it, she told herself. It was no dream, but contact from the other side. Fully awake now, Eileen turned on the light to look at the bedside clock: 1:30 A.M. With a shiver she wondered about the R-101. Where was the airship now? How was it doing? Was it still flying safely on its path to India, or had something already happened?

She wished then that she had never been able to see into the future. Because then she wouldn't know about the fate of the airship. She wouldn't hear the screams of the passengers and realize she couldn't do anything to prevent the tragedy from occuring.

She could only lay awake in her bed, gripped by a terrible fear, and wait.

"We're Down!"

Inspection took longer than he expected.

Harry had to walk over two miles of girders and catwalks inside the cavernous belly of the ship to get to all five engine cars. It was the first time he had been inside the dirigible at night while she was in operation. It was a strange feeling. The dim lights cast a strange glow inside the forest of wires and lines, and the throbbing of the diesel Tornadoes echoed eerily in the cathedral-like space.

Harry kept a steady grip on his flashlight as he navigated the narrow catwalk. He felt like an acrobat, but at least his rubber-soled shoes helped him maintain solid contact on the ladders and gangways. All the officers and crew were instructed to wear light tennis shoes as part of their uniform to prevent damage or sparks. With so much hydrogen on board they had to take special precautions.

Harry popped out of the mid-engine gondola to

check the giant hydrogen cells that filled the main portion of the airship interior. Filled with the gas that kept the R-101 in the air, the sixteen bags stood as high as ten-story buildings. They were jammed into the girder structure like a row of huge bass drums. But Harry was shocked when he saw the gas bags. The violent jerking of the aircraft during the storm caused the bags to surge and sway. The thin coverings on the bags were rubbing directly against the metal frame of the ship. If this continued, the rubbing would tear holes in the bags, releasing the precious gas and making the aircraft too heavy.

Harry took one last worried look at the bags before he climbed into the hull to get back on deck. It was now 1:45 in the morning. The inspection had taken well over an hour, but at least he was confident that all five engines were performing well. There wasn't anything he could do about the bags at the moment. Still too tense to sleep, he returned to the smoking room. This time it was empty. He fixed himself another tonic water and lime and sank into the wicker sofa.

The R-101 was battling across northern France in the very center of the storm. Harry gripped his glass as the ship jerked against the blustery winds and sleet. At one point the nose of the ship tilted and the ship seemed to fly vertically. A cushion slid off the sofa. Harry laughed nervously as he reached down to pick it up.

A steward from the two o'clock shift poked his head in the door.

"Can I get you anything, sir?"

"How far are we from Paris?" Harry asked.

"Just coming over Beauvais, the next town to the south, forty miles northwest of Paris," the steward told him, then continued on his rounds.

Once again he was alone. Harry felt another jerk and stared out the rain-splattered window. They were flying too low. The R-101 skimmed dangerously close to the top of a church spire and the side of a factory.

"Pull up, pull up!" Harry exclaimed in alarm.

Without warning he found himself sliding down the length of the sofa, toward the forward bulkhead, until he came to an abrupt stop. A bottle and several glasses on a table near him slid to the floor and shattered. Then the table itself skidded down the polished floor.

The engine room telegraph rang. It was just 2:05 A.M. Harry heard it clearly in the lounge. He scrambled to his feet and rushed to the window. What he saw made him widen his eyes in horror.

The R-101 was approaching the base of a hill, moving slowly but directly toward it. Even as Harry's heart pounded in fear, he felt the nose of the big ship sink down.

We're going to crash! he thought.

Just before they hit, he clutched at the white heather and thought of Clare.

Fire in the Sky

There was a sickening crunch.

The lights went out.

A brilliant burst of flame lit up the doorway. Harry fell to his knees when the ceiling of the smoking lounge collapsed. There was the sound of a loud explosion, followed by a rumbling and a crashing noise. If the hydrogen cells ignite, we'll all be dead, he thought.

Get out, get out, get out! an inner voice commanded.

Acting on reflex, Harry crawled toward the lounge wall. He clawed at the thin canvas. Finally it ripped open and he jumped through the burning dirigible, landing in the branches of a tree. Dazed momentarily, he dangled in the air, barely taking in the sight of the smoking dirigible below.

There were two more explosions and the entire structure ignited. The once majestic shape of the 777-foot airship burst into flame, crumpling like an accordion within seconds. Harry heard the agonized screams of fellow crew members and officers, as well as those passengers who had awakened. Trapped inside their quarters, they vainly struggled to escape the flames that roared into the night. People from the village were running to the site of the crash, but stopped short when confronted by the inferno.

I have to help my friends, Harry thought.

He jumped out of the tree and landed with a thump on the ground. He got to his feet and hurriedly examined himself. Apart from superficial burns on his arms and slight cuts, he was miraculously unharmed.

Harry heard voices coming from the area of the engine gondolas. He raced toward the tail section and found two of his engineers, Arthur Bell and Joe Binks, crawling away from the inferno. They had been saved by a ballast tank bursting over their heads at the moment of impact and dousing them with water.

"Thank God you've made it!" Harry cried.

Apart from surface burns, they seemed to be fine. Perhaps other passengers and crew were as well.

Two men from the village rushed over to join them. One was English, the other French.

"Come and help!" Harry shouted. "My friends are burning to death!"

With the two other men he ran back to the ship, hoping and praying that others could be pulled alive from the wreckage. But it was too late.

Only six people survived the crash and the inferno, including Harry. Fifty-four people had boarded the R-101 when she took off on her great adventure at 7 P.M. Major Scott, Sir Sefton Brancker, Secretary of State for Air Thomson, and forty-five others were dead.

Harry realized he couldn't do anything further to save his friends and fellow officers. He sank on the wet grass and covered his face with his hands. He wanted to block out the nightmare. But the yellow-orange flames raged beneath his eyelids. His heart was raging, too. He was aware of his ragged breathing, his pounding chest, even the feel of the crumbled ash that landed on his exposed face and hair. I must be in shock, Harry told himself. But I'm alive, he thought, dazedly. I'm alive. . . .

Within a short time the crowd of villagers were joined by the local police and the 51st Infantry, arriving in ambulances, horse-drawn carts, and trucks. The cavalry arrived, too, carrying piles of bedsheets. Harry grimaced as the soldiers walked around the still-smouldering wreckage and draped the bodies with sheets.

So many people dead. So many hopes for the

R-101 gone up in smoke. The future of airships lay scattered and burning on the ground in pieces around him. Harry got slowly to his feet. He would have to find a phone or a wireless operator to get word of the crash to the Air Ministry in London.

Harry felt along the front of his jacket and was surprised to find the sprig of white heather still attached to his lapel. But first, he had to call Clare. He wanted to be the first to tell his wife that he was alive and coming home to her.

The Dead Commander
Speaks

On October 5, 1930, all of England was in shock over the crash of the R-101. The rest of the world was, too. Paris lowered its flags to half-mast and *The New York Times* devoted a full front page to the story. When the dirigible went down, the exact cause of the crash went with it. No officers survived to piece together the tragic last minutes of the flight.

Eileen Garrett thought otherwise. Heartsick over a crash she had foreseen yet could not prevent, she arranged a session to try to make contact with any spirits from the R-101. I'll do it for Sir Arthur, as well, she vowed. Surely the Sherlock Holmes in Sir Arthur would have wanted to solve this last great mystery.

Four people were invited to the event, among them Harry Price, a famous psychic researcher known as the Ghost Hunter. Price let Eileen use his laboratory on the top floor of the London Spiritualist Alliance. At three in the afternoon on Tuesday,

October 7, the session officially began.

Eileen sat in an armchair facing the rest of the group across a table. One woman took out a notebook and pencil, prepared to take notes. Eileen took a deep breath, closed her eyes, and got comfortable. *Sir Arthur, if you're here,* she silently intoned, *please help me establish communication with any of the dirigible's deceased officers.* Breathing deeply, her head slowly fell back against the back of the chair. In less than five minutes she had fallen into a deep trance.

Eileen became agitated. She began to cry, and clutch and unclutch her hands. Her mouth opened and a masculine voice came out.

"I see a man named I-R-V-I-N-G or I-R-W-I-N," she said.

The name of the second officer in command of the R-101 was Irwin. The woman taking notes began writing furiously as the voice continued.

"He says he must do something about it . . . apologizes for coming . . . for interfering . . . for heaven's sake, give this to them . . . the whole bulk of the dirigible was entirely and absolutely too much for her engine capacity. Engines too heavy."

The words flew faster and faster. At times the technical nature of the terms confused those at the sitting, but all were recorded carefully. The voice continued: "Also let me say this . . . Explosion caused by friction in electric storm. Flying at too low altitude and could never rise. Load too great for long flight."

After fifteen minutes of details, the voice stopped. Eileen slumped in her chair and became silent. But then, surprisingly, another presence made itself known through Eileen's Arabic control, Uvani. "I sense an elderly person here. He is tall, heavy, has difficulty in walking. Jolly. Great heart. Deep blue eyes. Drooping mustache, strong chin, dominating, courageous, heart of a child." The accented voice of Uvani paused, then became clipped and British-sounding. "Here I am, Arthur Conan Doyle. Now, how am I going to prove it to you?"

The new presence brought everyone in the room to attention. Quickly getting over their initial shock, the members of the group began tossing questions out at the author, asking him about his books and his life. At the end, the spirit of Sir Arthur Conan Doyle discussed his feelings about mediums, and about one in particular. "But within one certain medium there is pure gold. She is sitting here and I hope everybody will understand we are good friends. . . ."

The flow of words stopped. Eileen remained still for several minutes. Gradually, her breathing changed and she began to wake up, as if she had been lightly dozing. She looked around the room.

"Did anything come out about the R-101?" she said.

"That and much more," Harry Price declared with a twinkle in his eye. "But first let's discuss the R-101 material."

Eileen read the transcribed notes passed on by the spirit of Captain Irwin. Although Eileen wanted to make the revelations public as soon as possible, Harry Price advised waiting until the hearings at the Court of Inquiry were over. Reluctantly, Eileen and the others agreed with his decision. Then Eileen was handed the notes from Sir Arthur Conan Doyle's conversation. Reading over the writer's last comments, the personal message to her, Eileen's lips curved in a private smile. "We *are* good friends," she softly said.

Epilogue

On October 30, the ghost story took an unexpected turn. Eileen received a phone call from an acquaintance named Major General Sorsby. Sorsby informed her that someone connected with the Air Ministry had received a telepathic message from his former colleague Captain Irwin of the R-101. The message had disturbed the Air Ministry official, but he was anxious to arrange a session with Eileen to learn more.

On the evening of October 31 at seven o'clock, Major Oliver Villiers arrived at Eileen's apartment and the sitting began. Once again contact was quickly made with the spirit of Captain Irwin. This time the deceased captain recounted the entire story of the doomed dirigible's last hours. The sitting lasted more than an hour, and toward the end included the voices of Navigator Johnston and Major Scott.

Major Villiers was so impressed by the session with Eileen that he immediately scheduled two more. At these, as well, he learned facts and information that only the designers or pilots of the R-101 could have known. Armed with what he viewed as substantial evidence, Major Villiers offered the transcripts of the sessions to Sir John Simon, the presiding judge at the Court of Inquiry.

Despite the facts contained in the transcripts, Sir Simon wouldn't allow the evidence to be admitted in court. After days of testimony, the exact cause of the dirgible crash was never determined. Various theories were proposed, however. A large section of the envelope could have torn off during the storm over northern France, exposing the gas cells to the rain and wind and causing hydrogen leaks. The structure of the giant ship could have been too large to fly in winds higher than forty miles per hour and snapped in two under the strain.

Harry Leech was acquitted of any blame or responsibility for the crash. The court found that his engines had performed admirably. Privately, he swore that he would continue to investigate the cause of the crash that had killed so many of his friends and colleagues.

Eileen Garrett continued to explore her unique powers of telepathy and clairvoyance by studying with respected physicians and psychiatrists. She traveled abroad and to the United States to lecture and participate in scientific experiments. Two of her greatest dreams were realized when she moved to New York after World War II and established the publishing house Creative Age Press and the Parapsychology Foundation in 1951. Despite all the activities of her later years she never forgot the victims of the downed R-101. When she died on September 15, 1970, she was considered one of the most respected and well-known mediums of the twentieth century.

The explosion of the R-101 was one of the worst disasters in British aviation history.

After October 5, 1930, no rigid airship ever flew over England again.

Recommended Reading

Botting, Douglas. *The Giant Airships*. Virginia: Time-Life Books, 1980.

Collier, Basil. *The Airship History*. New York: G.P. Putnam's Sons, 1974.

Croall, David. *Fourteen Minutes: The Last Voyage of the Empress of Ireland*. New York: Stein and Day, 1979.

Cross, Wilbur. *Ghost Ship of the Pole: The Incredible Story of the Dirigible Italia*. New York: William Sloan Associates, 1960.

Deighton, Len & Schwartsman, Arnold. *Airshipwreck*. New York: Holt, Rinehart and Winston, 1978.

Flynn, Michael. *The Great Airships*. New York: Carlton Books Limited, 1999.

Fuller, John G. *The Airmen Who Would Not Die*. New York: G. P. Putnam's Sons, 1979.

Hayes, J. Gordon. *The Conquest of the North Pole: Recent Arctic Exploration*. New York: The Macmillan Company, 1934.

James, Gilbert. *The World's Worst Aircraft*. New York: St. Martin's Press, 1975.

McKee, Alexander. *Ice Crash: Disaster in the Arctic, 1928*. New York: St. Martin's Press, 1979.

Robinson, Douglas H. *Giants in the Sky: A History of the Rigid Airship*. Washington: University of Washington Press, 1973.

Toland, John. *The Great Dirigibles: Their Triumphs and Disasters*. New York: Dover Publications, 1957.

Zeni, David. *Forgotten Empress: The Empress of Ireland Story*. London, England: Halsgrove, 1999.